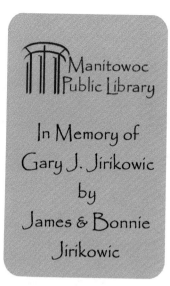

THE
SECRET
LIVES
OF
FISHERMEN

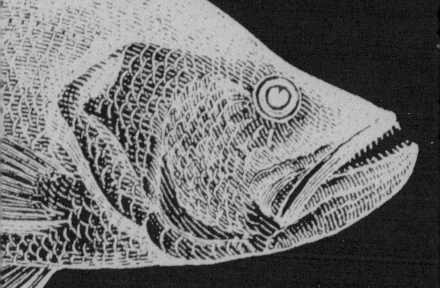

THE
SECRET
LIVES
OF
FISHERMEN

MORE
OUTDOOR
ESSAYS
BY
JIM DEAN

The University of North Carolina Press

Chapel Hill & London

© 2000

The University of

North Carolina Press

All rights reserved

Manufactured in the United States

of America. Designed by Richard Hendel

Set in New Baskerville and Champion types

by Tseng Information Systems

The paper in this book meets the guidelines for

permanence and durability of the Committee on

Production Guidelines for Book Longevity of the

Council on Library Resources.

Library of Congress Cataloging-in-Publication Data

Dean, Jim, 1940–   The secret lives of fishermen :

more outdoor essays / by Jim Dean.   p. cm.

ISBN 0-8078-2580-8 (cloth: alk. paper)

1. Fishing—North Carolina—Anecdotes.

2. Hunting—North Carolina—Anecdotes.

3. Dean, Jim, 1940–

I. Title.

SH531.D43   2000

799.1′09756–dc21   00-027313

04   03   02   01   00

5   4   3   2   1

For my children, Scott & Susan

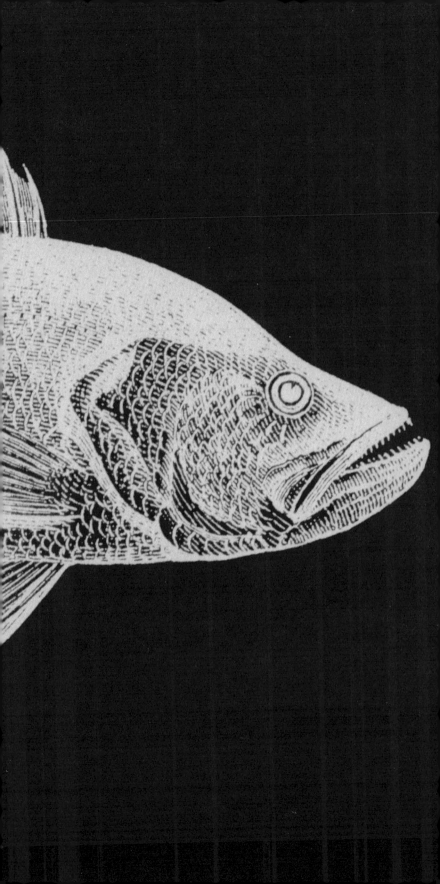

CONTENTS

PREFACE

When I took early retirement as editor of the North Carolina Wildlife Resources Commission's magazine *Wildlife in
North Carolina* in October 1998, one of the things I looked
forward to—besides fishing more often, of course—was having time to gather the material for another book. I had in
mind something similar to *Dogs That Point, Fish That Bite*,
which was published in 1995 by the University of North
Carolina Press with the support of the Wildlife Resources
Commission. That book, now available in paperback, is a
collection of fifty "Our Natural Heritage" columns written
for the magazine.

The Secret Lives of Fishermen includes 39 more of these columns selected from the nearly 250 I've written since 1979.
(I'm still writing the column, by the way, thanks to my old
boss Sid Baynes, chief of the Wildlife Resources Commission's Division of Conservation Education, and my longtime
associate Larry Earley, who replaced me as editor.) Also included this time are seven longer pieces chosen from free-
lance features I've written for various outdoor magazines
since 1964. Two of these—"The Pointer of No Return" and
"Confessions of a Chicken Chaser"—were revised from essays that first appeared in *Field and Stream* in September
1986 and April 1987, respectively. "Fishing Cars and Hunting Trucks" draws on one of the columns and a longer piece
in the February 1986 issue of *Field and Stream*. "The Bird at
Hand" first appeared in the September–October 1997 issue
of *Shooting Sportsman*. "Crazy Fishing," "Little Alligator Summers," and "Country Store Gourmet" were all published in
Wildlife in North Carolina.

The essays in *The Secret Lives of Fishermen* loosely follow the
chronicle of a year because that's how those of us who love
the outdoors tend to keep track of time. The title notwithstanding, you may note that not all of the essays are about

fishing, nor are you likely to discover any shocking secrets, unless you're surprised to learn that most fishermen and hunters don't measure success by the number of fish caught or animals killed. Some of the stories are linked to my experience (or rather inexperience) running a family farm, and others are admittedly nostalgic memoirs that celebrate traditions and natural resources that seem to be disappearing.

Occasionally I am asked whether the events I write about are based on actual happenings. Did, for example, my father put a shock collar around his own neck and ask my mother to test it on him to make sure it wouldn't hurt his bird dog? Did my brother and his family truly find live wood ducks in the stoves at my cabin at the farm? Have my friends and I really fished for largemouth bass using lures with no hooks? Yes, all of these stories are largely true, although I confess that I have embellished some accounts and occasionally taken liberties with the actual sequence of events.

Many of the companions who have shared these adventures with me are not fishermen, or at least they are not men. Among them are my daughter Susan, as well as several close friends, including the wives of some of my male fishing buddies. They don't seem to care that the word "fisherman" is inherently sexist, but I realize that others might. The editors and I considered substituting "angler," but that word has acquired a faintly elitist flavor that seems out of place when describing someone sitting on a bank soaking worms under a cork. Someone suggested "fisher," but a fisher is a member of the marten family, an aggressive mammal that hunts in our northern states and Canada. "Fisherperson" just seemed silly, like "cowperson" for "cowboy." So we've generally stuck with "fisherman," and we hope you will not find this offensive.

I would like to express my appreciation to the many fine folks I've worked with at the Wildlife Resources Commission and to the good friends who have shared their humor and inspiration on countless outdoor adventures. They are a remarkably patient bunch, frequently putting up with more than they bargained for and then, worse, having to read about it later. Finally, I'd like to offer special thanks to all who have read these essays through the years. If we still haven't gotten around to wetting a line or following a dog together, perhaps we will. I would like that.

THEODORE
GORDON
ON
TOBACCO
ROAD

This will mark the second opening day following the death, at eighty-eight, of my old friend A. J. Johnson. Somehow, this year I suspect he will be missed more than ever when the rest of us gather at his mountain cabin for the traditional start of the trout season. Last year, I think we tried to pretend that Johnson was still there, just momentarily out on the porch watering the plants. But now it is sinking in that he has not simply gone for a walk up the stream, nor is he in the kitchen stoking the fire in the wood cookstove, sneaking red peppers into the oyster stew, or stirring a highball with the tip of his forefinger, as was his custom.

Though I am fortunate to have been a part of this annual celebration for some thirty years, time is changing the characters, if not the plot. Once we were the youngsters happy to throw our sleeping bags on the bare floor and wash all the dishes. We were the ones who rushed out to the stream at first daylight to beat the water to a froth. Now we're the old-timers who harass the new kids and get to sleep in real beds—even if that happens to be alongside the snoring champion of Forsyth County.

But we all share one priceless gift from our departed friend: Johnson taught us to fish for trout in these remote and tumbling streams, and in doing so, he marked us for life with a healthy disrespect for some of the contrived notions that seem to afflict those who view fly fishing for trout as high religion. In the early years, before Johnson got hold of us, we were newly obsessed by the sport and convinced that trout could be caught only by those who worshiped the two-headed God of Extravagant Equipment and Immaculate Imitation.

Oh, we were insufferable. We studied aquatic entomology, tied thousands of flies, raised our own roosters, bought the latest high-tech rods and reels, waded boldly, waited for nonexistent hatches, fished far and fine, and spent countless hours discussing hydrology, light refraction, and color perception. If Theodore Gordon, Francis Halford, G. E. M. Skues, Ernie Schweibert, or Lee Wulff wrote that it was so, then it was so. And like most evangelicals, we preached to the unwashed and sought converts everywhere. In short, we consumed everything on the table except the main course.

Naturally, Johnson would laugh at us and wade out into the icy stream wearing rotten canvas shoes while fishing with an old seven-and-a-half-foot glass fly rod and a six-foot level leader so stout that he could barely poke the end of it through the eye of a size ten, well-gnawed dry fly with half of its hackles unwinding. He usually fished a Wulff Royal or a Blonde Wulff because it floated well and he could keep track of it on the swift currents. And he would invariably catch the most, and biggest, wild browns. It tore us out of our sanctimonious frames.

Johnson also frequently fished a sinking fly—usually a black ant—on a tippet below the dry fly and introduced this deadly tandem tactic to guides in Idaho, Montana, and Wyoming in the early 1970s. Those who have since written enthusiastically about this technique in books and magazines probably have no idea that it can be traced to the dark hollows of the Southern Appalachians.

It took a while for most of us to realize that Johnson was not making fun of the use of reasoned tactics or practical observance—he was just much better at it. He had long since learned that what might be true of trout in a New York Catskill stream, a Pennsylvania limestoner, a brawling Montana river, or even a southern tailwater didn't necessarily apply in the small, clear, nutrient-poor freestone streams of the Southern Appalachians. Wild trout in these waters starve if they don't eat darn near everything all the time.

Thus, there is no southern Theodore Gordon propounding a canon on the selective feeding habits of trout precisely because he'd be a damned fool to do so.

And if wild trout in these waters often feed opportunistically—there are always exceptions—they more than make up for it by being the spookiest creatures on the planet. I think wild browns can hear a car door slam a mile away, and they will run like dirt-road lizards if they see you or in any way sense your presence. Furthermore, they usually stay spooked the rest of the day. Thirty years ago, in a moment of supreme frustration, I wrote that wild trout in our streams would eat anything we couldn't get close enough to feed them. Johnson liked that, but it wasn't an oxymoron for him.

One day when we had been alternating pools—he was catching trout, I wasn't—he finally pulled me aside. "Lemme see what you're using," he said. "That ain't no good —leader's too long, fly's too small, and you're fishing the wrong spots." Oh, is that all, I remember thinking. Then he showed me one of his tricks.

He waded into the whitewater at the head of a pool I'd already fished and reached out to gently dap his fly on the swirling eddy at the opposite edge of the current. He was hidden by the foam, and as the fly drifted, it was engulfed by a wild brown nearly fifteen inches long.

"Sometimes the only way to fish a good spot is from straight overhead," he said with a grin. Like the old goat himself, it was simple, practical, effective, and he loved it all the more because few fly fishermen would be caught dead doing it.

HOME
IN
THE
RANGE

With an afternoon hike behind them and the sun dipping into the trees, my brother and his family were no doubt thinking of supper and an evening fire as they walked through the barren fields and up the dirt road to the old tenant house we use as a rough camp. It had been hot in the direct sun, but winter is treed only temporarily in early March; it waits to pounce from any shadow. Nobody was thinking about the strange noises they'd been unable to locate in the cabin earlier.

John was getting ready to chop some kindling, while Beth and the girls, Jessie and Melissa, began to cook supper. It was Melissa who lifted the eye of the wood cookstove.

"Dad," she said calmly. "There's a duck in the stove."

And so it was. Obviously, it had come down the chimney, crawled through the flue and down the six-inch pipe, and then somehow squeezed past the damper into the back of the stove. A handsome—if somewhat sooty—male wood duck peered back at them from the narrow draftway between the oven and the side of the stove. John captured it gently, and after everyone had admired it a moment or two, he carried it out on the back porch and turned it loose. It flew off.

Oh well, they thought, that was curious. After all, by the time most ducks get into a stove, they've been plucked and stuffed with apples and celery—their presence as a dinner guest is never by choice. But things were about to go from curious to downright strange.

Having successfully extracted the duck from the Home Comfort in the kitchen, John decided to ward off the evening chill by building a fire in the Franklin stove in the front room. He wadded up some newsprint, piled up some kindling, struck a match to the paper, and closed the fire door. Moments later, there commenced from within a clamorous flapping.

He flung open the fire door and a female wood duck, à la flambé, fell out in a shower of burning kindling. John said he could almost imagine it wiping a singed brow with a wing and saying, "Sufferin' succotash, it was getting hot in there!"

While Beth doused the scattered embers, John did what he could to snuff out the flaming duck. Since the duck was understandably agitated, he quickly carried it to the porch.

"I never knew a duck could run so fast," he said. "It made a bee-line a hundred yards through the field and hit the pond at a dead run." John swore he heard a "pssssssssssh . . . ahhh" when it plopped into the water.

At this point, you may be wondering why ducks would fly down a chimney and sit in a stove. Believe it or not, it's perfectly natural. Unlike most ducks, which nest on the ground, wood ducks normally nest in hollow trees much the same as squirrels and some owls. They usually begin looking for nesting sites sometime in February or early March. The eggs hatch in the spring, and the young ducklings climb out of the hollows and plop safely to the ground or water, sometimes from heights of twenty feet or more.

Early in this century, wood duck populations fell to critical levels when favorable nesting sites were lost to extensive logging in hardwood bottomlands. Beavers had also been virtually trapped out, and their ponds provide prime wood duck habitat. Furthermore, until 1934, wood ducks were subject to market hunting for the millinery trade. During the past twenty years, however, the placement in the wild of thousands of wood duck boxes by waterfowl hunters and other conservationists has helped restore favorable nesting habitat. Beavers are also back—amid considerable controversy—and they've clearly helped return wood ducks to prosperity. Indeed, these handsome ducks are now the most common waterfowl species in most southeastern states, including North Carolina.

But despite the profusion of nesting boxes and beaver ponds, an open chimney still looks a lot like a hollow tree. It's not difficult to believe that woodies investigating the chimney on our cabin might have thought they'd found a "for rent" sign on Graceland. Here was housing with a formal entrance leading to a hallway between two rooms. And talk about location; it even had a pond in the backyard. How were they to know someone would set fire to their bedroom?

The truth is that lots of wood ducks are attracted to chimneys. Ask Mike Gaddis. A few years ago, he built a log cabin with a stone fireplace. One day the following spring, he unlocked the door and stepped inside. Pictures were off the wall, lamps were knocked over, soot was everywhere. A female wood duck sat in the middle of the floor looking at Mike as if to say, "Sorry about the damage; just put it on my bill."

As for us, we're taking our property off the market by placing a grate over the top of the chimney. If we decide to cook a big pot of soup next spring, we'll bring our own quackers.

BACK
TO
BLUEGILL

About two years ago, Jay Wheless called me from Manteo and, after introducing himself, shocked me with the following: "You've written about an old millpond called Bluegill where you and your grandfather used to fish. From your descriptions, it sounds like the same place my family bought some years ago." We quickly established that it was indeed the same place, and while I was pondering this remarkable coincidence, Jay made a generous offer: "Would you like to go back and fish there sometime?"

Of course, I said yes, thinking how wonderful it would be to see the old thirty-three-acre pond where my grandfather, W. S. Dean, had taught me to fish when I was eight years old. Over the winter, I spent a good bit of time thinking about a return trip and trying to decide when I had last been there. I would have certainly fished there with my grandfather in the fall of 1967, but he died the following March and I could recall going back only once the following summer with my dad, William Graham Dean. Within a year or two, the property had been sold and the surrounding timber clear-cut. I had heard—wrongly, as it turns out—that even the old cabin and boathouse had been torn down. Over the intervening years, Bluegill and the happy, heedless summer afternoons I'd spent there had grown ever distant.

But Jay's offer was proving irresistible, calling up old memories of Sunday afternoon fishing trips, my grandfather still wearing his "go-to-meeting" white shirt, coat, and tie and smelling faintly of fried chicken and yeast rolls and not so faintly of Muriel Senators. I remembered the occasional bass we caught, especially a big one Granddad landed one brisk autumn day using his Pflueger Supreme reel, split-cane Heddon casting rod, black linen line, and Creek Chub crippled minnow.

When I was ten years old, I'd hooked my first big bass there—big, to me, anyway, though it weighed only about four pounds. That fish struck a silver South Bend Nip-I-Diddee, and I recalled the tense moments as I played it through a stump garden until I got it alongside the boat. I can still see it lying on its side in the dark water, my grandfather reaching out with the landing net, and the small bead swivel that simply, inexplicably, pulled apart. And I can see the bass drifting slowly down in the dark water—still unaware that it was free—until my silver lure was just a glimmer.

So this past year I looked for an opportunity to take Jay up on his offer, and I asked my father to come along—I was, you see, already sentimentally thinking of this as a three-generation reunion. One unseasonably warm day last March, Dad and I drove the familiar fifteen miles from his home, covering the last few miles down a gravel road to the gate. A hundred yards farther, we crested a ridge and saw the cabin and boathouse with the lake beyond, dark and inviting, just as they had been in the past, or nearly so. We looked around for a while, sharing recollections. I stuck my grandfather's old felt fishing hat on Dad's head and took his picture, then we went fishing. We caught a few bass. Dad hooked one that gulped his floating lure right beside the boat in hot mid-afternoon while he was picking out a backlash. And somehow I chanced to catch a four-pounder just before dark. Symbolically, it was the perfect match for the bass I'd lost forty-seven years ago. But something was missing.

Though much was the same, a great deal was different. The countless familiar stumps throughout the pond had long since rotted away, the dam had been rebuilt, the trees hadn't fully regrown, and everything looked somehow smaller. It was all a dreamy, skewed vision of what I remembered, the reality somehow less tangible than the memory. And now that months have passed, I am aware of something else. What I saw in March has overprinted some of the older memories I had of the place, so I can no longer recall exactly how things looked years ago.

That was a risk I had anticipated. After all, I have steadfastly refused to visit the houses I grew up in because I want to remember them precisely as they were when I lived in them. As for Bluegill, it will always be one of my favorite places on earth. But the Bluegill where Dad and I spent a very enjoyable day this past spring belongs to Jay and his family and their more recent memories. It is in good hands, surely, but my grandfather wasn't there that day. He and Dad and a pimply kid are in an old wooden skiff among long-gone stumps where there is a bass with a silver Nip-I-Diddee in its mouth.

REALITY
BITES
ON
TREES

The storm that howled across the farm last fall could have been much worse. It peeled up the corners of tin roofs and carried away plastic from the plantbed greenhouse, but the damage was quickly repaired. We weren't quite sure, however, what to do about one large old apple tree in the orchard. It lay on its side through the winter, but when buds appeared on it this past spring, we decided it might be possible to save it.

One afternoon in early April, Curtis looped a chain around the trunk and slowly pulled the tree upright with the tractor. His wife Louise and I struggled to screw a steel anchor rod nearly five feet into the ground, then rigged a cable from the rod to the tree. When the cable was securely clamped, Curtis eased the tractor back a foot or so and I unhooked the chain.

If we didn't break too many roots while setting the tree upright, it should bear apples, but I'm afraid I have become too much of a fatalist to begin counting September's pies. My history of tree stewardship hereabouts is by no means heroic.

Trees are planted by hopeful people. The assumption we make is that we will get to sit in their shade, eat their fruit, enjoy their beauty, or sell their timber at some point in the distant future — or our children will. A person who doesn't make plans at least twenty or thirty years down the road is not likely to go to the trouble. When I first took over as manager of our family farm some dozen years ago, one of my dreams involved trees. I saw towering cypress along the

edges of the ponds and catalpa trees overrun with those
fat worms beloved by bluegills. I pictured groves of black
walnuts and orchards of pears, apples, peaches, and sour
cherries along the dirt lanes. I saw willow oaks, maples, and
redbuds in the yards. One area seemed ideal for a pecan
grove. Grant Wood never painted a more perfect landscape
than the one I thought would someday bear my signature,
and though I never expected to live long enough to see all
my efforts mature, I certainly hoped to watch them grow.
At least I could imagine a grandchild looking up into a
dense canopy someday and saying, "My granddaddy planted
these."

I got busy right away, ordering saplings and studying the
proper planting methods. I dug holes big enough to bury
Buicks, watered, mulched, pruned, sprayed. I waded into
the icy ponds in winter and planted cypress. For several
years, progress was satisfying. Then things began to happen.

A grove of fifty walnuts failed in the third year. Pecans
simply wouldn't live where I thought they should despite
several replantings. Fruit trees were nibbled to death by
deer or dried up in hundred-degree Augusts during severe
droughts that took a heavy toll on even hardy trees like
maples and redbuds. Oh well, I thought, I can buy fruit, walnuts, and pecans at the market. I did have a few successes.
A handful of cypress survived the nips of beavers, muskrats, and cattle. The catalpas are coming along, and after
two replantings, several cherry, peach, and apple trees seem
likely to make it. When I stop to consider all the trees I have
planted, I can understand why Mr. Wood chose to render
his visions in oils on canvas rather than on actual land.

It doesn't help that the two spindly maples Curtis yanked
out of the woods and stuck in the dirt in front of his house
have prospered beyond all belief and now shade his porch
with lofty thirty-foot crowns. Or that he gives me a knowing wink every time he remarks on their progress. Nor does
it seem fair that in pastures and fields left fallow only two
years, pines have volunteered with such ferocious enthusiasm that they can barely be bushhogged.

Clearly, I have a lot to learn about silviculture. Meanwhile, my carefully tended conscriptions look as though they might be serving life without parole in Job's garden.

I suppose you could say that I simply don't have a green thumb, but it seems more basic than that. Out of the many trees I have planted, this spring I could count less than a dozen still living. Only a single tree stood out as a resounding success. It was a cypress I planted at the edge of a pond ten years ago. It had soared to fifteen feet, and its trunk had swollen at the base admirably. I half expected to see little cypress knees poking above the dark water any day. Encouraged, I gave the tree more attention than usual, placing a wire cage around it for protection and weaving Spanish moss into its limbs.

Every time I fished the pond, I looked fondly at my cypress. Every time, that is, until one day in mid-April. The water was very high because a new family of beavers had moved in and dammed up the spillway yet again. As I prepared to cast toward the bed of lily pads beneath my lovely cypress, I gasped. Where was my tree? It didn't take long to finger the culprit. The water had risen above the wire cage, and a beaver had gnawed off the tree at the waterline. My dream had become a rodent's toothpick.

It was not a very subtle reminder, was it? We often think we are in control, and some of us live a lifetime with such illusions. But we are fooling ourselves.

I don't think I'll be planting any more trees right away. But I may ask for volunteers.

THE NEWS FROM WASECA

Spring is here, or soon will be. You can tell by the catalogs that bloom in the mailbox. Wordsworth, a daffodil man by all accounts, would not have liked it, but these days, he'd be just another occupant. Most of us could probably do without most of these mail-order harbingers, but I do miss one catalog.

For many years, until the company bit the dust in the mid-1970s, I looked forward to receiving the annual inch-thick catalogs from Herter's of Waseca, Minnesota. Many readers will remember them fondly. Recently, I ran across an old copy and spent several nostalgic hours reading it.

Each Herter's catalog had a distinctive red, black, and yellow cover inscribed with a coat of arms. In its typical quirky way, the company described itself as "the authentic world source for fishermen, hunters, guides, gunsmiths, law enforcement officers, tackle makers, forest rangers, commercial fishermen, trappers, explorers, expeditions, backpackers, precious gems for investors, couturier silks, and hobby crafts." It was all that and much more.

Founded in 1893, the company specialized in fully equipping expeditions to Hudson Bay or other remote parts of the globe. The range of products was truly astonishing and included guns, tackle, archery gear, taxidermy equipment, decoys, boats, motors, snowmobiles, and even exotic foods, candle molds, and teddy bears. If you wound up in some out-of-the-way place like Nepal or Minto Flats, Alaska, you could order everything you needed, then spend the winter reading the catalog.

Reading was the fun part. Unquestionably, George Leonard Herter and his remarkable family were experienced and widely traveled sportsmen with useful insights and knowledge. But to hear him tell it, he had invented nearly everything, including items any discerning reader would recognize as pure rip-offs. George also apparently wrote almost all of the pompous, grammatically fractured, and wonderfully weird copy that accompanied the ads.

He loved to disparage competitors' products and regale readers with outrageous claims and strange, truncated facts. George didn't merely sell a hat; he force-fed you his history of hats. In an ad for golf clubs, he stated that "they really have not been changed except by Herter's since King James II of Britain in 1457." His ad for an electric shaver boasted that it had "no gimmicks like bars that are supposed to roll whiskers into slots which is impossible to do if you just stop to think about it."

Throughout the years, George could never decide whether his company was singular, plural, possessive, or incorporated. Thus, one encounters the oft-repeated motto, "Herter's Have Tomorrow's Products Today."

But where else could you order Herter's famous buffalo chip candy or Herter's authentic cactus Sioux ghost dance candy? Or Hudson Bay North Breeze aftershave lotion, which "contains a real deodorant that really deodorizes." Or a cast-in-sand iron corn bread maker hawked in copy that traced the development of iron to Leif Eriksson. Or Herter's authentic sperm whale harpoons for use as fireplace tools. And who wouldn't want one of Herter's wild rice Benedictine fruitcakes, which "contain no trash fillers like orange peel and citron as used in present day fruitcakes"? Especially since George added thoughtfully, "We do not try to make any money on them." As he would say, "Order one out."

George also wrote many books in the same slapdash style. Who could resist *How to Get Out of the Rat Race and Live on $10 a Month* or the three volumes of *Bull Cook and Authentic Historical Recipes and Practices,* which, he claimed, included the favorite recipes of everyone from Jefferson Davis to Genghis

Khan? But George wasn't always full of beans. His book on fly tying is still highly regarded. It sold for $3.27 ($4.37 for the deluxe edition).

Prices were reasonable, sometimes downright cheap. Amazingly, quality was often very good, though a bit uneven. Throughout the 1960s and early 1970s, I ordered most of my fly-tying materials from Herter's, and I built several glass rods for as little as $4 from Herter's components. I still use some of them. For a surprisingly modest price, you could put together your own custom rifle with a fine English-made Mauser action and legendary Douglas barrel and a high-quality gunstock of myrtlewood, bird's-eye maple, or fancy fiddleback French walnut. Those lovely stocks ranged from $15 to $85.

In recent years, the Herter's name has been revived for a line of waterfowling gear, but the catalog is not the same. If you ever encounter one of the originals, read it and shed a tear for the demise of the grandest mail-order missive of them all.

CONFESSIONS
OF A
CHICKEN
CHASER

I was reading about Dame Juliana Berners recently. She's the English nun who is thought to have authored the first essay on sport fishing, "The Treatise on Fishing with an Angle," published in the second *Book of St. Albans* in the fifteenth century. She is also credited with developing some of the first basic trout fly patterns. Little is known about Berners, but I suspect the other nuns considered her a bit strange.

I have this mental image of her sitting solemnly at vespers when suddenly she hears a flutter of wings high overhead in the chapel. A starling flies to its nest, and a raucous chirping erupts as it feeds its young. Despite the separation of nearly five centuries, I think I know exactly what would have passed through Berners' mind at that moment. Her upward gaze might have been mistaken for religious fervor, but there's a better chance that she was soon alone at her fly-tying vise while somewhere around the abbey, a rumpled starling missing a few breast feathers and primaries had acquired an increased wariness of box traps and bird seed.

As a longtime fly tier who has also spent considerable time in the company of other fishermen who tie their own flies, I know a little about the obsessive nature of this hobby. Winding that first hackle is like probing a bear trap with your foot. It begins so innocently. Anyone who develops more than a passing interest in fly fishing, especially for trout, salmon, or bass, is likely to want to learn to tie flies. It seems to be a useful hobby that can give you something to do during the off-season, and most novices have the impression that tying flies can save money.

What happens is that you buy a few basic tools and materials and set out with modest expectations to tie a few flies in those patterns you use most often. The small cardboard box that holds your fly-tying equipment is replaced by successively larger boxes, and within six months, you are very likely to find that you cannot stuff your accumulation of hooks, furs, and feathers into any container smaller than a dumpster. Which, by the way, is one of the two places your significant other has suggested that you stuff it.

By this time, of course, fly tying has passed the hobby stage and become a ruling passion. Worse, the thirst for creation cannot be slaked by simply acquiring materials through mail-order or tackle shop purchases. A major part of the pleasure is discovering new materials never before used to fool a fish. Once this search is enjoined, virtually everything becomes potential grist for the vise. If you live with a fly tier, this explains the missing dental floss, the balding horsehair shoe brush, the unseemly gap in the poodle's French cut, and kitty's lack of whiskers. It's as though giant moths are furtively nibbling away at the very fabric of the planet.

While I was in college many years ago, I made a trip with my friend John Killian to fish for smallmouth bass in the upper Potomac River. As I was rigging my fly rod, he handed me a fur-bodied streamer fly that he swore would be the undoing of any bronzeback that glimpsed it.

"I call it the 'Chinchilla Killer,'" he told me as we waded into the river and began to cast.

"I've never seen this fur in any catalog," I said.

"My mother has a chinchilla coat," he said matter-of-factly. Seeing my surprised look, he added a sheepish qualification: "I clipped it from around the bottom where no one would notice. But try not to lose the fly because there's not much fringe left."

As promised, the fly turned out to be a killer for smallmouth bass. I have not seen John in at least thirty years, but

I have wondered about that coat—it must be getting a bit thin under the arms too by now.

More recently, another acquaintance who always seems to have an enormous supply of natural furs explained his source. He travels a lot and always carries a hatchet, a skinning knife, scissors, and a supply of plastic bags in the trunk of his car.

"I suppose you could say that I run an asphalt trapline," he said. "I keep an eye peeled for roadkill. You'd be surprised how many creatures perceive that they have been born on the wrong side of the highway. It's easy to replenish my supplies of squirrel tails, rabbit masks, possum pelts, and deer hair, and I even find a few raccoons, muskrats, and beaver. Some people collect aluminum cans; I collect corpses. I figure I'm performing a public service."

Understandably, his wife doesn't share his enthusiasm. He doesn't gather fur when she's riding with him, especially since the day she was looking in the freezer for some lima beans and discovered a curious tinfoil package that turned out to be the complete, though rather flat, carcass of a partially decomposed red fox.

"She threw it out," he said wistfully. "Can you imagine? She chucked a lifetime supply of Light Cahill bodies, not to mention enough rare, urine-stained dubbing for several dozen Hendricksons."

This, by the way, is the same fellow I once accompanied to a knitting shop. "Lots of neat tying stuff here," he explained.

"I'm a fisherman," he told the clerk. "I need some bright yellow wool to use when I tie trout flies. You know, those bugs with hooks in them to catch fish. The yellow yarn makes a perfect egg sack on a fly called a Female Adams."

The clerk chewed on that with a look of bemused tolerance as she dug through the skeins of yarn.

"Are you sure you don't mean Eve?" she asked, handing him a sample.

"Eve?" my friend questioned.

"A Female Adam," she said. "That would be an Eve, wouldn't it?"

Small wonder fly tiers tend to seek mostly the company

of their own kind. Still, if you are under the impression that fly tying exists solely as a support system for serious anglers, you're wrong. Believe it or not, there are folks out there tying flies who do not fish, nor are they motivated by profit. The wife of one of my fishing buddies was so taken by the delicate beauty of salmon flies that she begged him to teach her how to tie them. Sensing a windfall, he encouraged her to take up the hobby.

"She hates fish," he said, shaking his head. "Doesn't like to catch them, touch them, or eat them—except for fish sticks—but she ties the most exquisite Jock Scotts and Silver Doctors I've ever seen."

That would have come as no surprise to the late Tom Loving. Chances are you have never heard of Loving, but if you fly fish for bass, you may be familiar with some of his creations. As a milliner in Baltimore in the 1940s, Loving had a superb stock of feathers and furs, and he began to tie innovative bass bugs for his friends. One of his friends was the late Joe Brooks, angling editor of *Outdoor Life* and author of countless magazine articles, as well as several watershed angling books that helped introduce a legion of fishermen to the joys of fly casting for trout, bass, and saltwater species. Brooks also pioneered fly fishing for bass on Currituck Sound back in the days when bamboo rods reigned. One of his favorite bass bugs, still tied and used by modern anglers, was the Marsh Hare. It was originated by a maker of women's hats who didn't fish—Tom Loving.

During the decades since I first wrapped a pipe cleaner around a hook and caught a bluegill, I think I've managed to keep my indulgence in fly tying pretty well under control. I tie patterns I need when I run short, and I try to keep up with promising developments. But I'm past the stage where I conduct twenty-four-hour tying binges or tie flies for fish I know I'll never encounter. I can also look at a chicken and envision it fried rather than "flied."

Indeed, my worst moment as a fly tier came at the hands, so to speak, of some chickens back in the early 1960s after one of my trout-fishing companions showed me a dozen rooster capes he had recently acquired. This was several years before Bucky Metz, the fly-fishing son of a poultry farmer in Pennsylvania, realized that one high-quality blue dun, grizzly, or ginger rooster cape might fetch more than a coop full of setting hens and began to raise roosters bred to produce fine hackles. Before Metz made fly-tying history, quality rooster capes were scarce items.

"Where did you get such lovely capes?" I asked my friend. "Most of mine are scraggly little imports from India."

He chuckled knowingly. "I drive out in the country and when I pass a farm where there are chickens in the yard, I stop and take a look. Most farmers will sell a rooster for a couple of bucks at most. I take the bird home, chloroform it, skin the cape off the neck and salt it heavily until it's cured. Go with me and I'll show you."

What could be easier, I thought, as we wheeled his family station wagon onto a winding two-lane blacktop the following Saturday afternoon and began to look for prospects. We had traveled no more than a few miles when we spied a magnificent rooster with ginger hackles that glittered like pure gold as it strutted in a field next to a farmhouse. Its saddles must have been eight inches long.

We pulled into the driveway and walked around back where we found the farmer and several kids loading a truck. In retrospect, we should have been more honest. We should have bargained only for the rooster and been frank about our intentions. But we were afraid our true purpose might seem silly.

"We're, uh, thinking of raising some chickens," I said. "We saw that rooster and thought we'd ask if you'd like to sell him."

"Well, sure," said the farmer. "I got plenty more'n I need, but you're gonna be needing some hens and maybe another rooster or two. You young'uns catch that big yaller rooster and some of them others. I seen 'em run under the house."

On the way back to town, we shared the front seat with a scurvy-looking leghorn that sauntered back and forth clucking and eyeing us with curiosity while half a dozen of her sisters in the backseat pecked out a fast cadence on the upholstery. In the rear of the wagon, the incredible ginger seemed to be holding his own against overwhelming odds.

Maybe Dame Berners would have understood—it's some consolation to think so—but it's no coincidence that I have not tied all that many flies in recent years.

THE
MARSHMALLOW
PURISTS

Maybe it's the fact that we are away from home and are over-come by the joyous anticipation of adventure. Or maybe it's because we can't resist the urge to redefine our identity in the presence of those who don't know us. Or perhaps it's just that, regardless of age, we are all still kids full of barely contained devilment. Whatever the reason, I have observed that the practical joke is never more tempting than when we gather with new companions to share our common obsession with fishing or hunting in distant places. The most even-tempered among us is very likely to become either predator or prey.

My friend Matt Hodgson, for example, pursues his ruling passion for fly fishing seriously, but like many who have been at it a long time, he sometimes grows weary of the near-religious pedantry and politically correct intolerance that he encounters among some anglers who have been newly baptized in the oft-contrived rituals of this sport. "It gets tedious," he observed as he told me this story.

On a recent trip to fish the Yellowstone River in Montana, he and his companions found themselves one morning in the company of a guide who seemed far too inclined to preach the gospel. "Now, I don't know how you fellows fish back home," he sniffed, "but here we fish only with flies and we release all trout. I would much prefer that you fish with dry flies, but if you have some other notions, we should discuss them."

Matt had hardly anticipated such a sermon. Not only is he unlikely to be taken for a rube, but his experience as a fly fisherman and fly tier far exceeded the guide's.

"Well, to tell the truth," Matt replied, "what I had in mind was a technique we prefer back home in North Carolina. Why don't you fellows go on ahead, and I'll run back into town and get about two hundred yards of stout cord and some 3/0 hooks. This looks like a really good place to set a trotline. You don't right offhand know where I could get a mess of chicken necks for bait do you?"

Sometimes the best way to crush a stereotype is to play to your adversary's worst fears. For a moment, the guide looked as though he had caught a bullet with his teeth, but when the laughter died down and he realized that Matt had no intention of stringing chicken necks across the Yellowstone, he relaxed and joined his peers for an enjoyable day of fly fishing.

Those of us bred and born in the brier patch of southern culture are frequently called upon to diffuse an unfortunate (or fortunate) stereotype when we travel to distant lands where our mother tongue is automatically linked with toothless ignorance and inbreeding. But sometimes it's fun to keep those suspicions alive too.

In the late 1970s, some friends and I journeyed to Pennsylvania to fish the storied limestone streams where Vincent Marinaro, Charley Fox, Ed Koch, and others had spawned a new and highly sophisticated technique for catching wild trout on flies carefully fashioned to imitate terrestrial insects. We had spent the winter tying flies, reading the literature, and preparing ourselves for this crusade to Mecca.

We drove all night and rendezvoused with our Keystone State guides on the stream shortly after dawn. They seemed a bit reserved, but they looked at our tackle and apparently decided that we at least looked like fly fisherpersons. My friends, however, were not about to let such an educational opportunity pass.

As we tromped down to the water, we swapped those precious bits of information that are thinly disguised to reveal our knowledge and establish our credentials. Fly boxes were shared and patterns compared. Just when it looked as though we might be accepted, one of the Pennsylvania anglers asked to see the patterns I'd been tying for this occasion.

Proudly, I produced my fly box and flipped open the lid. Each compartment was filled with tiny marshmallows, sorted by color—white, pink, yellow, green. I was stunned. The Pennsylvanians looked like someone had slapped them with a wet carp.

"But . . . but," I stammered.

"Yep," said one of my North Carolina companions. "We should have warned you, I suppose. Dean, here, can match any hatch with a marshmallow. Fishes them dry too."

The worst of it was that my Tar Heel buddies had emptied my several hundred flies into a paper sack—it took hours to get them sorted out. But everyone—well, almost everyone—had a good laugh and another stereotype had bitten the dust. We had a grand time fishing together that week.

And one of us had colorful snacks to eat on the stream too.

SPORTUGUESE
AND
METAPHOR-PFISHING

The language of fishing is colorful and often carries complex and confusing baggage. In that sense, it's like the jargon or technospeak that accrues to any special-interest group. We tease those who work in government or the military because they rely on a virtually impenetrable insider's lingo, but we're all guilty. You want jargon? Take up sailing, skateboarding, snow skiing, or golf. For that matter, follow any spectator sport like baseball. "Sportuguese" is the first language a reporter who covers these activities must learn, but arcane shoptalk is evident in everything from cooking to carpentry.

Call me a jargon junkie, but I particularly like to collect examples of the unique gibberish that surrounds my favorite sport. Among bass fishermen, for example, a voluminous idiom has flowered simply to describe a backlash. A backlash is what happens when the spool holding the line on your fishing reel revolves too quickly during the act of casting, causing a tangled wad of line to blossom and jam the reel. It can achieve epic proportions, and, what's worse, it's a regular occurrence.

Fishermen seldom call them backlashes, though. Instead, we resort to metaphors. "Dang it, I got another bird's nest," I will say. My friend Jack Avent more often uses the term "bouffant," as in "Ain't that a lovely bouffant?" He will say this as he shows me a reel that has sprouted such a massive wad of monofilament that it appears to have been styled with a hair dryer. Of course, it is not uncommon for these terms to be preceded by a string of adjectives.

A more sophisticated term for a backlash is "professional

overrun." This implies that the tangle is unavoidable and occurs only among highly skilled fishermen. Indeed, the act of announcing a backlash can be so creative that it approaches an art form. A longtime fishing companion—was that you, Jack?—swiveled around in his seat one day and presented his reel for inspection.

"What's that called?" he asked innocently as he displayed a truly awesome snarl.

"What's what called?" I answered.

"That," he persisted. "What do you call it when you get a mess like that?"

"You mean a backlash?" I replied, unaware that I was being set up.

"Oh, so that's a backlash," he mused. "I've heard of those."

If there are innumerable ways to describe such a simple mishap, they pale in comparison to the vast number of terms used to describe what a fish does when it is fooled into sampling a lure or bait. Furthermore, these terms can vary depending on the type of fish or tackle. "I had a strike," a fisherman will announce. The term "strike" is commonly used to indicate that a fish has attempted to intercept the lure but has somehow avoided becoming hooked. Fishermen may also say they had a "hit," "tug," "tap," or "bump," these terms being more or less interchangeable with "strike," but they usually use these words only when fishing with artificial lures. "Bump" or "tap," however, may also imply that the fish didn't strike with characteristic enthusiasm. A relatively new term with a similar meaning is "push," as in "I felt him push it." This usually means a fish—particularly a bass—has taken only a halfhearted interest in your lure and has probably come up from behind it and either bumped it or turned away at the last moment. The experienced fisherman using a stiff graphite rod can often detect this, even if the fish never touches the lure. Vibrating plugs or spinnerbaits skip a few beats when the "pushed" water momentarily interrupts the lure's action.

These interpretations can be subtle. For example, if you say you had a "bite" or "nibble," you're probably fishing with some type of natural bait. No, I don't really understand the distinction either, but ain't it fascinating?

Wait, it gets worse. If you say that you've had a "rise," you're probably using a fly rod and fishing with a floating fly. And the fish is almost surely a trout (though possibly a carp) since trout delicately rise to the surface to sip your offering while rambunctious fish like bass are more likely to, as one friend puts it, "knock the snot out of it."

In recent years, it seems to have become fashionable in classy sporting magazines to use the term "eat" anytime the writer wishes to indicate that a fish has had a tactile encounter with an offering. It's arguably more universal in application and probably expresses the fish's intentions, but it seems affected to me. If a fish were to "eat" one of my lures, I would expect to see the lure swallowed and digested, and I'd just as soon that didn't happen because then I'd have to buy another one.

My favorite of these wild and crazy expressions, however, is one I read years ago. When the late Clare Conley was editor of *Field and Stream* in the 1960s and early 1970s, he published a list of some of the more imaginative descriptions he'd seen in the countless manuscripts that had crossed his desk. The one I remember best was submitted by a hopeful author who was apparently looking for a way to avoid a cliché and at the same time describe the contemplative prelude to a strike.

"I could tell the fish was interested because he was making little investigative bulges around my fly," he wrote.

Priceless, isn't it? Funny thing is, every fisherman knows exactly what he means. We've seen lots of those "little investigative bulges"; we just didn't know what to call 'em.

THE
LAUGHING
PLACE

"I don't know exactly what happened," my old friend told me. "It just wasn't the same anymore. Somehow, I got burned out."

"But that was years ago," I said. "Don't you ever get the urge to go again?"

He shrugged his shoulders. Here was a person who had once confessed that he loved fishing so much that he was unable to sleep the night before a trip. In fact, fly fishing for trout had become such an obsession that he had gone out West after college and gotten a job as a guide. After two years of fishing such storied streams as the Madison, Henry's Fork, and Big Horn, he quit and came home—gave away his tackle and hasn't wet a line since.

"I got too close to it, I guess," he said. "After taking people fishing from dawn to dark every day through two seasons, not to mention fishing for my own pleasure every spare moment, I realized that I no longer looked forward to it. Came to almost dread it, in fact. I know it sounds odd."

Maybe it doesn't. Over the years, I have known others who bellied up too close to the fire and stayed there too long. Part of it must inevitably come with the passing years, a maturity—if you can call it that—that tempers youthful enthusiasm. I've had similar feelings about some of my life-long passions. And yet I know older people who have managed to nurture an interest throughout their lives. How do they do it? One of them once told me that the secret is to hold the things you love at arm's length. "Sip, don't gulp," he said. "That's the way to keep your hobbies always fresh."

That advice seems to apply to the love of places too.

Thirty years ago, I had a near-desperate desire to live within sight of a trout stream. Or to have a place at the beach where I could walk out to the end of my pier, get into one of several boats—while you're dreaming, you might as well dream big—and fish to my heart's delight. Or I thought I could be happy living beside a lake or on a farm surrounded by good ponds. I never really could decide which appealed to me most, but since all of those notions were unobtainable at the time, I didn't have to decide right away.

In the intervening years, I have managed to gain access to some of those places, at least on a modest basis. I bought a few remote acres on a small trout stream in the mountains and rented a tiny cabin nearby. I fixed up an old tenant shack at the family farm and worked on the irrigation ponds to improve the fishing. I now have the opportunity to live at the beach if I want to, but I haven't moved permanently to any of these places. I'm not sure I will. It may seem ironic, but I care too much about them.

I think of what Uncle Remus said while relating his tales of Bre'r Rabbit: "Everybody's gotta have a laughing place." He understood quite well that everyone sometimes needs an escape, but you can't escape to a place if you already live there.

Several years ago while driving up the dirt logging road to my mountain cabin after an absence of some months, I realized that if I lived there, a time would surely come when it would no longer be a thrill to drive leisurely up that creek and see the tumbling rapids or admire the foliage turning amber after autumn's first cool snap. Instead, I would hurry along that all-too-familiar route, eyes straight ahead, thinking of chores or complaining about the washboard ruts. All that beauty and opportunity might easily become too familiar. With a stream at your doorstep, its pleasures are so accessible that it's too easy to put them off until tomorrow or next week. Then one day you realize you haven't fished in months, years. Is it our nature to embrace obsessions so heartily that we crush them beyond recognition?

Visiting your laughing place should be an adventure. You anticipate and plan, choose your companions, pack up the gear, and head out on the road. Or you do it on the spur of the moment.

"I'll bet you'd enjoy going again," I told my friend. "You know, just a little sip. Enough time has passed."

"Well, if you want to show me one of your laughing places this spring, maybe I'll go with you," my friend said. "At least I wouldn't have to guide."

"I know a spot," I said. "You might even catch a few bass, and if you're having fun, I promise we'll quit while we're ahead."

"You mean you'd leave while they're still biting?" he asked.

Some folks never learn.

VIRTUAL
FISHING

You may not be ready for this, but here goes. The goal of some fishermen these days is not to catch fish. Furthermore, the best are those who don't catch the most fish. If you're thinking this sounds like one of those newfangled, sensory-manipulating computer games, you're wrong. These are flesh-and-blood anglers fishing real water, and many are highly skilled professionals who compete in tournaments. Most are trying not to catch bass, but some concentrate on not catching walleyes.

Been there, done that, you say? No, no. You and I may not catch fish on some of our trips, but we never set out with that in mind. We want to catch fish; that's the whole idea. Not so with these anglers. The more fish they don't catch, the better they like it. Good heavens, I'm making a botch of explaining this. Maybe I better just tell the story.

Two of my closest friends—let's call them Phil and Jack— are serious largemouth bass fishermen, and Phil occasionally even competes in local catch-and-release tournaments. They're constantly refining tactics, and one day last summer, I was invited to join them on what they called a practice trip.

"You won't need that net," Phil told me as I carried my gear down to the dock.

"Probably won't need your tackle box, either," added Jack.

"But I've got all my lures in there," I protested. "Oh, I get it. You've got a secret weapon you're going to loan me."

They just smiled, and after we crossed the lake to one of their favorite spots, Phil handed me a deep-running crank-bait.

"Wait a minute, somebody took the hooks off this one," I said.

"That's right," said Phil. "It isn't supposed to have any." That's when I noticed the other rods in the boat. All were rigged and ready. None of the lures had hooks.

"Okay, guys, a joke is a joke," I said, laughing. "I suppose the next thing you'll tell me is that we're actually going to fish with these things."

"We are," said Phil. "Tomorrow, I'm going to fish a tournament on this lake, so you and Jack are going to help me. I want to find out where the bass are and what they're most likely to hit, so we're going to fish a variety of lures, types of cover and depths until we find concentrations of bass, especially larger bass."

"But we don't want to actually catch any bass because that might give them the sore mouth or run them off the cover," explained Jack. "By using lures that have no hooks, we can still detect strikes, but we won't really disturb the fish. In fact, sometimes we can even get an idea how big a bass is if it holds onto the lure long enough. As soon as we get several strikes — enough to determine that bass are using an area — we back off quietly and go try another spot."

"If we're lucky, we'll have half a dozen good spots pinpointed before we quit today," said Phil. "Tomorrow, unless conditions change drastically, I should be able to come back to these same places and find fish."

"And then the lures will have hooks, right?" I said.

"You got it," said Jack. "And just to keep it interesting today, we've got a little $10 wager going. The one who gets the most strikes wins the pot. Hey, fishing without hooks is no big secret. Everybody is doing it."

Everybody? I looked around. Bass boats were trading back and forth across the lake, and at least half a dozen had stopped to drift over deep points and submerged humps or roadbeds. Off to our left, several boats were positioned to fish a flooded forest of standing timber, and others were working along shorelines or probing the edges of willows at the backs of coves. Two nearby boats were apparently waiting for us to leave our spot.

"Nobody in any of those boats is using hooks?" I asked in disbelief.

"Probably not," said Phil. "Not if they're competing tomorrow and certainly not if they know what they're doing."

So here we all are, fishing prime structure for obliging bass in balmy weather on one of the best largemouth lakes I know. But we're not catching; we're simply fishing. And this is how we'll spend the next eight hours until we tally our takes back at the dock. Still, as the saying goes, I seen my chances.

"I just now had a couple of hits," I announce casually. "Bumped it twice. Felt like a good fish too. Um, there he was again."

Phil and Jack exchange suspicious looks, but I ignore them. They may be better fishermen, but they're playing to my strength. Besides, I know where $10 will buy a fresh tuna steak.

CRAZY FISHING

Most fishing trips are pretty ordinary. We catch something or we don't, and either way, we return home largely content, having nourished our obsession yet another day. When Izaak Walton wrote *The Compleat Angler* 345 years ago, he recognized that there was far more to fishing than fish, and he called his favorite pursuit a contemplative recreation. Alas, his discourse does not divulge whether his angling ever gave him more to contemplate than he anticipated—or appreciated. Certainly mine has.

There was that time, for example, when one of my casts wound up in the creek behind a pond's dam, having traveled all the way through the drainpipe. Now that was something to contemplate. Some of my catches have also been a bit unusual. Then, too, there was that business that took place in a roadside ditch, when . . . well, I'll get to that later.

The drainpipe incident took place years ago on an unseasonably warm winter afternoon. Given the time of year, I had no great expectations, but I thought I might be able to dredge up a bass or two in a nearby pond by fishing a weighted plastic worm in the deep water along the dam. Besides, it was a pleasant day to be out. After going nearly an hour without a strike, however, I sat down opposite the drainpipe and began casting methodically, reeling very slowly. One other fisherman showed up, but he wasn't catching anything either.

I was daydreaming when I felt the unmistakable thump that signals a strike. I immediately opened the bail on my spinning reel to let the bass take the worm before setting the hook. Line poured off the spool. Boy, that was one fast-moving fish. When it showed no signs of slowing down, I closed the bail and set the hook. Nothing. Must have dropped the worm, I thought. I didn't think the bass had felt the hook, so I opened the bail again just in case. Line streamed out of the guides, faster than ever. By this time, the other fisherman had walked over to watch. I set the hook a second time, but there was no resistance.

"How come your line is going into that drainpipe?" he asked.

"It can't be in the pipe," I answered. "I didn't even cast in that direction."

"Looks like it to me," he said. I looked closely, and it certainly appeared that my line went directly to the top of the pipe, which was level with the water's surface. I began to reel, and after what seemed an eternity, the worm popped out of the pipe. The fisherman eyed me for a moment, then gathered up his gear and left.

I sat for several minutes trying to figure out how such a thing could have happened. Finally, I made another cast and watched in amazement as the mystery unraveled. A light breeze slowly blew the floating coils of loose line toward the mouth of the pipe. The line drifted across the top of the pipe and lodged against a bit of trash. I began to reel and shortly saw my worm climb over the lip and plop in. That plop had been my strike. I opened the bail, and somewhere deep in the bowels of the dam, my plastic worm yanked yards of line off the reel as it raced down the pipe and into the creek behind the dam. I went home, where I eyed myself suspiciously in the bathroom mirror.

Looking back, I can see a similar logic at work behind all the strange events that have happened to me while I was fishing — there's never been any inscrutable cosmic mystery, just relentless coincidence. Consider that summer day some years ago when I was surf fishing. The fishing wasn't very good, and after reeling in to check my bait — it was untouched — I set the rod in the sand spike and walked up the beach a short distance to stretch my legs. I didn't at first connect the woman's scream with the tight arc in my spinning rod. I thought a fish had grabbed my bait in the backwash of suds, and besides, the woman was fifty yards down the beach chasing a poodle.

I ran to the rod and grabbed it, at which point I noticed that my line ran straight to the dog. I had never, until that moment, considered that a poodle would eat a raw shrimp, especially one with a hook in it. My instinctive reaction to set the hook wasn't without benefit since the dog, slowed by the drag, proved easier for the woman to catch on its second run (for what it's worth, poodles don't fight much, and this one didn't jump even once). There was nothing to do then but give them both lots of slack line and await the consequences. Fortunately, when the lady arrived with my catch, I was able to get the hook out without using pliers. While I listened attentively as she made some suggestions to me, her poodle ate the rest of my shrimp. Hearing of the incident later, one friend commented that this was a prime example of why fishermen should always carry a gaff.

Another interesting catch was far less traumatic, but it fits the pattern. Almost no one used a fly rod in saltwater thirty years ago when I walked out one summer day on the Fort Macon jetty to try my new nine-foot, ten-weight rod equipped with a three-hundred-grain, high-density shooting head. Friendly fishermen gave me room to cast, curious to see whether I would catch anything, especially since no one seemed to be having much luck soaking bait or casting lures. I doubt they'd ever seen anyone use a fly rod in saltwater. After about a dozen casts, I had a solid strike on a Lefty's Deceiver streamer fly that I had been working slowly along the bottom.

"Got one," I said, in case someone might not have noticed. The fight was strong, though sluggish, but whatever I had hooked ran off to one side a short way, then reversed direction. It did this several times, giving me cause to suspect that it was most likely a flounder or spotted sea trout. You can imagine my surprise when I slid a size ten-and-a-half low-heeled canvas tennis shoe onto the rocks. It was hooked in the tongue, which was not only appropriate but also provided the fulcrum that had caused the shoe to plane first one way and then the other. It had been a convincing performance, and we all looked at the shoe for several stunned moments until finally one of the other fishermen found the right words.

"You oughta cast back out there," he said. "Them kind normally run in pairs."

Fishermen have been catching footwear—mostly old boots—long enough for it to become a cartoon cliché, but bagging the wahoo of the genus struck everyone as being nearly unique. The same, as I was soon to discover, might be said for appliances.

Not long after I caught the tennis shoe, I was fishing for flounder on the Emerald Isle Pier with some of the regulars I had come to know over the years. We each tended several rods baited with live jumping mullet in the slough just off the beach, and occasionally we would check a rod by reeling up the slack to see if we still had bait or if we could feel any resistance that might indicate that a flounder had eaten the minnow. As I was doing this, I felt the line tighten. I set the hook.

"Got one," I said (this is an egocentric habit that clearly needs to be broken). The rod bent sharply, and everyone rushed to the rail to see what I had hooked. It was soon obvious that this was no flounder because we could see a wide, silvery flash now and then as the fish darted back and forth several feet down in the green water.

"Looks like a bluefish, or more likely a big pompano or jack," someone said. The drop net was lowered, and everyone waited while I struggled to gain line. Moments later, the chrome-plated top of a drinking fountain cleared the water and was dutifully netted and slowly hoisted over the rail. It hit the pier with a resounding clang. The hook was caught in the drain hole in the center of the fountain top, causing it to slip-slide back and forth. I don't recall precisely what was said about this catch, though there may have been some mention of a rare hybrid between a horseshoe crab and a squid that propels itself by squirting water.

I have had other experiences that, while they don't defy explanation, are clearly cause for contemplation. Mike Gaddis and I were bass fishing one day when we pulled up to a likely looking stump. I cast to one side of the stump, and he cast to the other. He caught an eight-pound bass.

"I know why you didn't catch this fish," he said as he admired his catch, then turned it around for me to see. "Look here."

The eye socket — the eye that would have been able to see my lure — was empty.

As for the incident involving the roadside ditch, it occurred back in the 1970s when my friend Melvin Kennedy first began fly fishing for mountain trout. Though I was not much more than a novice myself, I offered to go with him and share what little I had learned.

"Trout aren't really hard to catch if you know how to read the water and determine which spots they like," I remember telling him, no doubt quoting some famous angling author. After reading the water over a two-mile stretch of river, Mel still hadn't caught a trout. And though he hadn't actually seen me catch one, he graciously allowed that he was certain I had. Discouraged, we left the stream and began walking back down the road to the camp.

"I think you must have a secret fly you're not telling me about," Mel said.

"No, really, I don't," I replied. "I haven't caught any — I mean, many — and there's certainly nothing magic about this fly. You just need to get the knack of letting your fly float naturally without dragging on the surface. A dragging fly spooks trout."

To illustrate my point, I stepped over to where a tiny spring run passed through a culvert under the road. The trickle was barely six inches wide and no more than an inch or two deep, except for a bucket-sized pothole under the end of the protruding culvert. With only a few feet of leader hanging from the rod tip, I lowered the fly onto the glassy boil.

"See, you need to let it float freely like this so that . . ."

Bam! A five-inch wild brook trout grabbed the fly and dangled quivering in front of us.

"Honest, Mel, I never . . . ," I stammered.

Mel looked first at the trout, then at me. Finally, he said what any fisherman would have said: "You're going to try to sell me that fly, aren't you?"

CLASSICAL
BASS

It is a simple image from a time when I was about ten years old, but it has remained clear all these years. I see this old glass-eyed, wooden Heddon Lucky 13 floating on dark water spangled with sunlight. If I had to guess, I would say it was one of my grandfather's bass lures and that the black water was the Little Alligator River. But it could have been the Chowan River, the Cashie, or Wiccacon Creek. It also could have been Jordan's Pond at Seaboard or Williams's Pond near Gatesville (now called Merchants Mill). Or it could have been one of the other old eastern North Carolina mill-ponds my grandfather and I fished together in the early 1950s.

Oddly, this half-century-old mental snapshot seems to have defined my fishing or at least the way I like to fish for largemouth bass. If you rummage through the clutter of your early angling memories, I'll bet you can find some similar moment or experience that has shaped your own angling preference. It's a subtle tug that isn't always obvious. In my case, it wasn't until fairly recently that I realized just how much those early experiences have influenced some of the choices I've made in recent years.

Like most serious bass fishermen, I have spent a lot of time during the past twenty-five years fishing big lakes like Kerr, Gaston, Jordan, Falls, and others in the North Carolina Piedmont—lakes that didn't even exist during my childhood. Construction of large lakes here and throughout the country was already under way prior to World War II, but the boom gathered a full head of steam during the decades after the war, setting the stage for vast changes in the way we fish. The Bass Angler's Sportsman's Society recruited many anglers, and manufacturers began to design vastly improved tackle and modern bass boats ideally configured to ply those big, open waters. With the advent of tournament fishing, the quest for largemouth bass became a national phenomenon with tournament pros and TV fishing show hosts becoming celebrities as well known as the top NASCAR drivers.

Many bass fishermen scorned the rapidly growing popularity of competitive fishing for prizes and money. Those who picked bones with professional fishermen argued that tournament fishing constituted the private use of a public resource for profit. It was also considered contrary to the gentle, contemplative nature of angling. Both are certainly valid arguments, yet the opposition is not nearly as strong these days, and for what may be a very good reason. Fairly early, professional fishermen began to take greater pains to ensure the release and survival of fish caught in tournaments, and they also began to preach the ethic of catch and release as an everyday practice. The TV angling hosts quickly adopted the same ethic. At first, cynics believed this was self-serving, economically opportunistic eyewash, and maybe it was. But a strange thing happened. The philosophy of catch and release began to spread. Nowadays, no self-respecting bass fisherman would think of keeping a fish, much less a legal limit. Indeed, the measure of a bass fisherman is how "big" a bass he can catch and then release. Ten-pound lunker? Back you go, big boy.

Even those who still disagree with the tournament approach have to admit that the celebrity factor has made catch and release the nearly universal ethic, and that alone has helped save a priceless resource. Bass fishing is better than ever in these big lakes because we're turning 'em loose. Furthermore, the availability of superior tackle and tactics is directly linked to skills honed on the tournament trail. Yes, the lakes are often crowded, and launching and loading can be a time-consuming pain in the butt. But this is one of those rare instances in which our worst fears were never realized. Quite simply, if you fish the big lakes, these are the good ol' days.

And yet for me, there's still that black water and that old

paint-cracked, perch-scale plug. I am pretty sure that most pleasures in life depend on some contrivance; surely my bass fishing does. Even sex, after all, is mostly a brain game. I love to fish those big lakes. I crankbait and Carolina rig the deep structure. I pig 'n jig and spinnerbait the brush. I catch some big fish because everybody does. But my soul is set on dark water Downeast fifty years ago, and that's where I am happiest.

Perhaps this partly explains why I canceled the order for a bass boat this year (though I may reconsider if it doesn't threaten my mortgage). It may also explain why I began collecting antique bass tackle years ago. It probably explains why I left the timber standing in a pond I built at the farm a few years back and why I have planted cypress trees and lily pads in all the ponds there. I am looking for something I misplaced years ago. And it doesn't have much to do with catching fish.

REVENGE
OF THE
SNAPPER

Anyone who spends a lot of time fishing or otherwise poking around on freshwater rivers, lakes, and ponds is sooner or later bound to conclude that the snapping turtle is appropriately named. One look at those fearsome jaws mounted on the end of the thick coiled spring that serves as a neck is more than enough to instill respect, even if you've never heard the old adage that those jaws, once clamped, won't open again until it thunders. Unless you're inordinately cautious, encounters with mature snappers tend to be memorable. Ask Phil Cable or Bill Williams.

Back before it became the centerpiece of a high-priced housing development, Sunset Lake was an old black-water millpond in western Wake County that occasionally yielded an outsized largemouth bass. Phil fished it regularly in an aluminum johnboat during the early 1980s, and on one of those trips, he spotted a large snapper that was busily churning up the bottom in shallow water, apparently feeding in a bluegill bed. As it rooted, the turtle's aft end and tail were exposed. Naturally, this toothsome sight made Phil hungry. Snapping turtles are good to eat, and here was supper. Furthermore, the tail was a convenient handle, indeed, the only safe one.

"I eased the boat over, grabbed the tail, and hoisted about twenty-five pounds of ticked-off turtle into the boat," said Phil. "I wedged it into the space between the transom and the backseat next to the battery. Then I went back to the front seat and resumed fishing. I could hear it scrabbling around, and it wasn't long before I noticed that water was rapidly filling the boat. That got my attention because I was a long way from the landing."

When Phil scrambled to the rear of the boat, he discovered that the snapper du jour had hooked one of its powerful claws into the ring of the boat plug and yanked it out. Equally disturbing was the fact that the turtle had backed into a corner over the open drain, where it was well situated to defend its handiwork.

"My only choice was to make a run for it," said Phil. "There wasn't a moment to lose."

Paddling furiously and running the electric motor wide open—a pitifully inadequate twelve-pound thrust—Phil headed down the lake as the boat settled lower and lower and moved slower and slower. With the seats practically awash, he finally managed to run the boat up on the bank just before it sank.

And the turtle? Phil ate it. After all, he was figuring on fishing Sunset again, and he didn't want to release his catch and take a chance that he might have to put up with a lot of snickering snappers when word got around.

As for Bill Williams, he has had a scar on his wrist since he was nine years old as a result of making a bad decision involving a snapping turtle—he thought it would be a wonderful idea to blindly poke his hand into a barrel holding a live one.

"It's the kind of thing you're more likely to do when you're young and trying to impress someone," he said ruefully. "We had caught this snapper and I had this sudden impulse to frighten my visiting first cousin by lifting this huge, ugly, hissing thing out of the barrel. I didn't look closely enough before I reached in because I was intent on watching her expression. I grabbed what I thought was the snapper's tail. When I lifted it out, I realized I had it by a foreleg."

The snapper quickly arrived at the same revelation with predictable results. Bill doesn't recall whether he had to wait until it thundered before he could pry the turtle off his wrist, but he admits he really wasn't paying too much attention to the weather.

Bill also witnessed another gruesome encounter with a

snapping turtle that took place some years ago on Santee Cooper.

"We were fishing for bass and heard someone hollering," he said. "We came around this point and saw a boat with a couple of fellows in it. One was down on his hands and knees yelling. Turns out he had caught a big snapper while crappie fishing. His first mistake was bringing it into the boat, but he made an even bigger mistake by trying to get the hook out. The snapper had clamped down on his index finger, and by the time we got there, the turtle had backed under a seat and dragged the fisherman with him."

"This poor man's partner was so scared of that snapper that he wouldn't help him," added Bill. "It was a pretty bad situation."

Yeah, but it could have been worse. The snapper could have reached over and pulled the plug.

THINKING
ABOUT
ANIMALS,
AND
VICE
VERSA

Do you look at your dog or cat and wonder what's going on in that head? Do you ask the same question about animals in a zoo? How about raccoons and squirrels that live in your neighborhood or wild creatures of all sorts that live throughout the world? What about birds or fish? Few subjects are more provocative and humbling than speculating about what an animal is thinking, or capable of thinking, yet we all do it.

Early one morning this past summer, I spent the night at the farm and was awakened shortly after dawn by a large, honking flock of resident Canada geese that flew into the pond behind the cabin to feed. That is, by the way, a wonderful alarm clock. They became a bit nervous when I walked out on the porch and then sat quietly in the rocker drinking coffee, but they soon settled down. After about thirty minutes, Curtis came up the path in his truck, and I thought the flock would surely fly. Nope. They seemed totally unconcerned. Curtis pulled around the cabin and stopped. The geese ignored the truck, even though some of them had fed up through the pasture and were quite near.

They're accustomed to vehicles, I thought, figuring that they must believe a truck is some sort of animal, like the cows they also ignore. Then Curtis got out of the truck. Instantly, the geese were in the air, honking warnings and heading for the horizon. If a goose thinks a truck is an animal, what must it think when an animal gets out of another animal? Wouldn't that scare the hell out of you? Did you see *Alien?*

This is quite normal stuff, of course. Deer aren't usually afraid of vehicles, nor are animals on the African plains. Indeed, squirrels aren't afraid of boats and will let you drift within a few feet, but they recognize the threat the moment you put one boot on the bank. What, we ask, must all these animals be thinking?

Our pets are a constant source of such wonderment. You interrupt your cat's nap to get something, dumping fuzzface out of your lap onto the floor. Yet even if you return immediately and pat your lap invitingly, does your companion forgive and hop up? Certainly not. It seems to sulk, and if you persist, the cat will stare into the distance as though you were not there. It seems to be so obviously ignoring you—a very human reaction—that you conclude the cat is thinking, "Okay, so you didn't want me then, you don't get me now."

Biologists warn us that this is dangerous ground, and they're right to do so. It's impossible to understand what animals are thinking, especially if we try to translate it into human terms. The accepted belief is that animals act most often on basic needs—hunger, for example—and that everyday functions are largely driven by instinct. The complex social functions of bees and ants are often cited as examples of instinct so refined that it camouflages itself as rational thought. Indeed, the scientific community continues to debate whether higher animals are capable of reasoning like humans. Can some animals encounter a situation, think things through, and evaluate options before making a considered decision?

Anyone who has owned, trained, and hunted with bird dogs or other sporting breeds would have no problem believing that dogs can reason. There are just too many occasions when no other explanation seems to suffice, although the evidence is purely anecdotal.

Haviliah Babcock, who wrote such wonderful books as *My Health Is Better in November,* tells a story about a bird dog that was so exceptional that Babcock thought he might be able to train it to retrieve two quail at the same time. The dog wouldn't do it. There were opportunities, but the dog refused to retrieve more than one bird at a time until, finally, one day Babcock shot two birds on the other side of a deep, water-filled ditch. The dog crossed the ditch and brought the first bird to the edge. Then it retrieved the second bird and laid it alongside the first. At last, thought Babcock, that dog is going to bring me both birds because it doesn't want to have to cross the ditch two extra times. But the dog found another solution. It ate one bird and brought Babcock the other.

Here's what I think, for what it's worth. I strongly suspect that many higher animals are capable of forms of reasoning, however primitive, that surpass pure instinct. My reasoning (if that's what humans do) is simply this: It's not that animals are human, it's that we are animals. No biologist is going to argue with that.

So your cat gets its feelings hurt and decides to punish you? Chances are you deserve it.

SHOULD MICKEY MEET VICKIE?

Have I told you about Vickie? Interesting character, Vickie. Like a lot of us, she's got a few problems. Of course, she doesn't talk about these things, but it won't hurt to tell you about them since Vickie isn't her real name.

Vickie's father left home before she was born, and nobody's seen hide nor hair of him since. He was a bit of a rambler, so nobody is really surprised. Actually, her mother hasn't been all that much better. She ran off with someone when Vickie and her sister and two brothers were still teenagers—left them pretty much on their own to raise themselves. Never sent any money.

Things aren't all that swift with Vickie's siblings, either. They never got along well, scrapping all the time. One of her brothers has a contagious disease that is sure to be fatal, and the other moved to the city and became a transient, begging food and raiding garbage cans just to survive. Well, he had always stayed out all night and slept most of the day, anyway. He could be a charming rascal, but you figured he could get mean in an instant. Wouldn't be a big surprise if he caught a bullet someday. Vickie's sister is likely headed for trouble too. Many think she's cute, but she's already got her brother's disposition, and she wears way too much eye makeup. Considering the company she keeps, it wouldn't shock any of us to find out that she's contracted the same disease her brother has.

I guess it's not any big surprise that Vickie has turned out the way she has. She's a piece of work, for sure, strutting around with this attitude that the world owes her a living. Bold is what some would call her. She wears real fur and couldn't care less what you think about it. And when she goes out with her eyes blackened halfway around to her ears, some say she looks like a raccoon.

Of course, that's because Vickie is a raccoon. And so is her rabid brother and the rest of her family. The story, as you probably guessed, is a fabrication; an example of anthropomorphism, which *Webster's Dictionary* defines as "ascribing human characteristics to nonhuman beings." The difference is that Vickie is not your usual Toonville type— certainly not cute—and the life described above is fairly typical for a real raccoon. There's nothing dysfunctional about her family either.

Humans have been anthropomorphizing for years, populating our entertainment, our advertisements, our entire culture with charming and utterly irresistible animal characters like Toad in "Wind in the Willows," Winnie the Pooh, Bugs Bunny, Mickey Mouse, and hundreds of others. It is so pervasive that we hardly notice it.

It's all in fun, we rationalize, and there's some truth in that. There would be a lot less laughter to share without the antics of Sylvester, Tweety, and the others. And surely we know that real animals don't think, speak, and act this way. Or do we?

Not only is it supremely arrogant of us to reinvent the universe in our image; it is confusing too. The danger of anthropomorphism is that it sentimentalizes wild creatures and tends to create an atmosphere that can lead to profound misunderstanding of their real lives and the interconnected roles they play in our ecosystem. Some people would go so far as to suggest that such cartoon characters also contribute to a growing ignorance of the nature of the human animal. Kids don't have to believe these cartoon characters are real to learn compelling—and dead wrong—lessons from them.

Have Elmer Fudd and the Big Bad Wolf helped teach us to despise all predators (including human hunters)? Is it partly Bambi's fault that so many people are sentimental about cute creatures—only cute ones, of course—in an ecosystem that has zero tolerance for sentiment? Did gentle Mickey foster the notion that nature cares what happens to individual mice? These ideas fly in the face of all biology, but they are surprisingly common these days, even among those who consider themselves highly educated. Have these lovable characters helped condition us to routinely confuse sound biology with moral choices? Is that why so many of us refuse to acknowledge that we humans are also members of the animal kingdom and—like it or not—are subject to the same irresistible forces of nature? Is that why eating meat, wearing fur, and hunting are social issues? Could be.

Unquestionably, it is far too late to rid our culture of anthropomorphic characters, nor is that necessary. But it would be a service to our education, and to the wild creatures around us, to find a bit more balance.

I believe Wile E. Coyote ought to catch a roadrunner once in a while and eat it for lunch. And maybe we should get Mickey a date with Vickie.

IS GETTING THERE ALL THE FUN?

Time for the annual summer-appreciation trip. I can't take you, of course, but I can tell you what it's like. The only real requirement is to travel through eastern North Carolina. You may wind up at the beach. Then again, you may not.

It's best to leave around 6:30 in the morning while it's still cool and the traffic is light. Head east and pick the back roads where you can drive forty-five miles an hour or less without holding up a long line of traffic. Roll down the window and listen to the buzz of insects in the fields and ditches as you pass. It's a nice sound, conducive to the state of mind you're seeking and something you wouldn't hear with the air-conditioning on and a tape in the deck.

Mood is important. Ideally, you want a relaxed, reflective sort of energy—the kind that follows a good night's sleep, two cups of caffeinated coffee (take a chance, for heaven's sake), and the anticipation of going. As silly as it sounds, the perfect song to have in the back of your mind is "Lavender Blue," the theme from *So Dear to My Heart*, that old, wonderfully sappy Disney movie about kids growing up in the summer on a farm. These times are not that simple, of course, but never mind. You're looking for a different kind of reality, remember?

It may help to think about how much you love your fellow man, but don't dwell on it. You'll too quickly find exceptions. Anyway, ignore any rudeness you encounter. You don't want this day spoiled by impatient drivers on your bumper, so let them pass. Put your body in first gear, your mind in overdrive, and roll on.

Look for passing postcards, perhaps a field of soybeans stretching away to a distant white farmhouse in a grove of ancient oaks. If you had many lives to live, you could spend one of them there. You know there are cicadas singing in those oaks. At noon, someone may sit in the shade and eat a platter of homegrown tomatoes in vinegar or turn the crank on a White Mountain ice cream freezer. Surely you recall the taste of homemade peach ice cream straight from the dasher and that it was your job as a child to poke your finger into the drain hole to keep the cold, salty water flowing.

Farther on, you pass a Victorian house set well back from the road at the end of a long driveway lined with cedars. It has a fine porch that extends all the way across the front of the house and halfway down the side. On it are wicker chairs, gliders with cushions, flowerpots, and ferns. Didn't you sit on just such a porch once? And in the evening, didn't you help shell butter beans and watch the fireflies while bullfrogs drummed in the ditch. Would we really need psychiatrists if we still spent our summer evenings in such company?

Wave at folks sitting on porches or farmers driving tractors. They'll wave back, if they didn't wave first. Admire the tobacco barns, count the cows, and see if you can spot just one mule. Check out the crops. Corn's a little dry, but the cotton looks good. Soon, there will be stray tobacco leaves and tufts of cotton strewn along the shoulders of the road and bales of wheat in the fields. We've lost autumn's picturesque stacks of peanuts and shocks of corn, though. Nor do you see much sugarcane these days. It began to disappear in the eastern part of the state after the war when sugar was no longer rationed. Who puts molasses in coffee these days or spoons it on a clabber biscuit the size of a catcher's mitt?

You don't have to spend the whole time driving. The following stops are authorized. You can pull off at a roadside vegetable stand or yard sale, wander through a flea market, or get yourself a vanilla milk shake. You can also stop at an old millpond where you might still be able to buy a bag of stone-ground cornmeal. While you're there, ask if the fish are biting. They did yesterday. Farther east, it is permissible to pause at any bridge crossing a black-water river. If the yellow flies aren't too thick, you might even want to take a short walk down the bank under cypress hung with Spanish moss. Take along a cold RC and pour a bag of peanuts in it.

You should be getting the hang of this by now. If you really are heading for the beach, you'll soon be passing huge flat fields where corn soars in long rows over the black soil. Somewhere along here, you will drop onto a beach that's 20 million years old, but you probably won't know it. Ranging south out of Virginia to Carteret County, the Suffolk scarp marks this ancient beachhead, and in some places, you can find fossil shells in the road cuts. Eventually, the dark earth will yield to sand, and you may imagine that you can smell the salt blowing in on a Bermuda high.

At this point, I suspect you will be more than a little heartened at the prospect of putting this miserable trip behind you. The kids are fighting in the backseat, the adults are no longer on speaking terms, the potato chips that fell down the neck of your shirt are beginning to itch, the dog has been hassling in your ear for three hours, and the air-conditioning is on the fritz. You see, dear hearts, I do live in the real world sometimes.

Ah yes, but if only . . .

LITTLE
ALLIGATOR
SUMMERS

The black-water run of the Little Alligator River isn't very wide where it passes under US 64 east of Columbia in Tyrrell County, but its cypress-rimmed shorelines spread rapidly as you head downstream into a huge embayment that joins the even larger mouth of the Big Alligator River. This is big water, almost invariably choppy, the color of steel, streaked with wind. On a clear day, you can look east across the Big Alligator and see the hazy, distant shores of Durant's Island and Dare County. To the northeast, only sky and water meet on the near-invisible horizon of Albemarle Sound.

On a late fall day in 1968, eight months after the death of my grandfather W. S. Dean, I helped my old high school friend Charlie Ogletree launch his boat near the US 64 bridge, then we ran down the Little Alligator and steered a course across its broad mouth until I began to pick out landmarks that were familiar to me. Several miles to the west lay the rotting remains of the old ferry slip at Fort Landing, so named, according to local history, because it had been a Confederate encampment.

"I believe that heavily wooded island back there toward Fort Landing is called Eagle Island—not sure you can distinguish it from the mainland at this distance," I said. "We always passed it when we came out here, and it had a massive nest in a tall, dead tree on the east end. It was probably an osprey nest, however, not an eagle's. We would leave the old ferry landing and run the three miles out here in a big juniper skiff loaded with all our stuff. Granddad's 4.5 Martin would barely move those heavy boats. It seemed to take forever, and sometimes we had to make several trips."

"How long has it been since you were last here?" Charlie asked.

"Not sure," I said. "Could have been in 1955, but probably a year or so after that." Charlie and I began to round a long grassy point, staying well off to avoid the shallow water I remembered.

"This low marsh is actually a small island," I continued. "There is, or was, a house, built on pilings like all the rest, that sat in a little gut on the back side of the island. The cats that lived their entire lives at that house and on its surrounding boardwalks had no tails; born that way, isolated like everything else out here."

"Up that way," I said, pointing north to a distant line of marsh, "is the entrance to a short winding creek not much wider than a skiff that led to what is called the goose pond."

Just around the grassy point, we entered a small, sheltered cove. Two of the cabins I remembered were still standing along the righthand shore, weathered sentinels crouched low on pilings over the dark water. They were little changed and were apparently being cared for and used by someone. We idled slowly until we came abreast of another cabin on the left, the one I had come to see. Charlie killed the motor and we drifted.

"That's it, isn't it?" he said.

I nodded. The main building—a central room, heated by a large potbellied stove, flanked by four small bedrooms and fronted by a screened porch—was window-deep in the water, and most of the deck and boardwalks that had once spread out around it like the white of a fried egg were long gone. The separate cookshack, dining room, and woodshed had a crazy tilt, half submerged, but the outhouse still stood like some ancient blue heron, looking as solid and ready for company as ever. We said nothing for a while.

"I wonder," I said finally, "if that old game of Chinese checkers is still in there?"

Charlie laughed quietly. "You're not going to try to go in and look, I would hope. Probably full of cottonmouths."

"Always was," I said.

In the early 1930s, my grandfather and some of his friends and associates in the cotton business took a long-term lease on this cabin just inside the hook of a marshy island on the north side of the mouth of the Little Alligator. They fixed it up, repaired the boathouse, added more boardwalks, and installed a Delco generator for electricity. Except for rainwater that collected in a wooden gutter and ran into a large barrel, all other supplies—ice, food, bedding, gear—had to be brought out each trip. For years, until they began to get too old, my grandfather and his friends gathered here to fish in the summer and hunt waterfowl and deer in the fall and winter. It was livable enough that Geneva and Graham, my mother and father, spent part of their honeymoon there in 1939. I once did the math to see if that explained my existence. It didn't compute, but it would have explained a lot.

My memories of this place begin a year or two after Dad returned from Germany in 1945. We would leave Halifax County hauling a dangerously overloaded trailer, cross the Cashie River at Windsor, and strike US 64 near Plymouth. Then we would head east across the Scuppernong River at Columbia and on to Fort Landing on a narrow road flanked by deep canals through seemingly endless swamp forests where it was not uncommon to see a bear. Even at age seven or eight—maybe especially at that age—I felt that we were leaving the known boundaries of civilization for a place mysterious beyond knowing.

It was an adventure filled with delicious possibilities. Maybe, I half hoped, a bear would charge. Or the trailer would catch fire—again. I had often heard the story about the time Granddad and his friends were on the last leg of the trip and noted with appreciation how friendly oncoming drivers seemed to be. They all waved and continued waving. Granddad waved back. Finally, someone noticed that the tarp over the trailer was on fire. Granddad quickly pulled over, but the flames rushed forward, threatening to engulf the trailer, which held not only all the tackle but also gas cans and shotgun shells. Bait buckets that could have been used to get water from the ditch were all under the burning tarp.

"Everybody out," Granddad ordered. "I'll drive fast enough to put it out."

Back on the road, he gunned his old Buick faster and faster past waving motorists, but every time he slowed down to check the status of the fire, it blazed higher and closer. Finally, it reached the gas cans and shells with spectacular results.

In desperation, Granddad backed the trailer into the flooded ditch. That saved the outboard motor and most of the tackle, but the blue paint on the trunk carried a speckled reminder of that event for as long as he owned the car, and I still have my father's old South Bend casting reel with melted knobs.

Alas, the family trips I recall lacked such invigorating incidents. Our guide would meet us at the small store at Fort Landing and help us load the skiffs for the near-interminable ride from the abandoned ferry slip out to the low marsh island and the cabin.

We shot our way in. With the skiffs cruising slowly past the cabin like ships of the line, Dad and Granddad would sit in the bows with .22 rifles and fire broadsides at sunning moccasins until the boardwalks were cleared for landing. Then we would unload the supplies, clean the rat droppings off every flat surface, and settle in for two or three weeks.

All those days are blended now so that many distinct memories are lost, but my mornings were always the same. At first daylight, I would awake to the distant drone of an outboard headed somewhere very slowly, a sound that entered consciousness so easily that you were not aware of it until it was annoying and you knew it would take at least that much longer—what, an hour?—to pass and entirely fade away. I would slip out the screen door and explore the wet boardwalks barefoot, shivering a little until the sun began to burn off the haze. I carried a cane pole to fish around the remnants of the boathouse or along the narrow boardwalk that ran to the outhouse. Periodically, the Delco would come on with a steady thump that recharged the batteries, but mostly I would have only mosquitoes and bullfrogs for company.

At sunup, while our guide was cooking a massive breakfast on a stove fueled by bottled gas, we would brush our teeth and wash up with lye soap in the cold water from the rain barrel. Even so, by the end of the first week, we would have established a more or less permanent patina of 6–12 insect repellent, suntan lotion, fish slime, dried sweat, and other varieties of exotic grime that no mosquito could penetrate or would want to.

After breakfast, the boats would be loaded for the day's trip. They were kept tied up alongside the dock, seventeen-to-nineteen-foot skiffs built solidly of juniper with foredecks and wide cowlings along gunwales that were stable enough to stand on. The skiffs were invariably painted gray, and no better or more seaworthy boat has ever been made for these waters. We didn't have electric motors then, but the boats handled so well that a person with a long pushpole could have walked one of them up the Amazon into the teeth of a cyclone. Though we fished in them almost every day, there was plenty of time to hang around the cabin shooting floating targets with a BB gun, playing Chinese checkers, or sitting back and exploring the huge expanse of sky and water. Day after bright day, it was the same. Breezes through the screens, the slap of water under the cabin floor, the hot buzz of insects in the marsh and bayberries, corks dancing on dark water, suppers in the cookshack with lamp-thrown shadows of ourselves on the rough, unpainted walls, and long sunsets until bedtime.

Sometimes I would simply lie on the dock and look into the brackish water, watching juvenile gar hunt small minnows among the pilings. But I tended to avoid the dark, back corner of the cabin where it nestled against the marsh after I ventured there one morning and found a huge snake with a body as big around as my thigh, its white belly bloating in the sun, still showing the water-bleached creases where a .22 hollowpoint had plowed through its coils. Where, I wondered, were those we had missed?

I didn't catch many fish, surely none of any size, around

the cabin. The real fishing took place in the skiffs. We would usually fish all day, carrying lunches and Granddad's old round metal cooler full of water, water that always had a peculiarly refreshing metallic taste when you poured it into the aluminum cap that also served as a cup. Often we would drift down the open mouth of the river for white perch, cane poles fanned out over the stern and baited with shrimp. Or we would anchor in the gut to the goose pond and fish for sunfish. The sunfish were mostly hand-sized redbreast sunfish—we called them robin—and pumpkinseeds. I don't recall that we ever caught bluegills.

Bradford Sutton was the guide who accompanied us most often. He was a big, jovial man, rough and friendly, and he and my Granddad often laughed at things that I'm pretty sure my brothers Graham and John and I weren't expected to understand. He would brag about our success at fishing, telling everyone that we had caught all the fish—we hadn't—and that no one he'd ever fished with was any better at it. He also showed us how to clean the sunfish and white perch, leaving the fins and tails on so that when they were fried, all you had to do was hold the fish by the tail and peel out the dorsal and anal fin bones intact. He teased Dad for stubbornly trying to cut them out before the fish was cooked. "Can't get them bones with a knife, Mr. Dean," he said. "Always cut some off and find them in your mouth. Too late, then, have to eat 'em. Do it the easy way." Dad, who never believed in the easy way, would keep sawing away until he delivered a pile of fish that looked like little otter-gnawed fishcakes that everyone else left on the platter.

It was Bradford who cooked and guided for Mom and Dad on their honeymoon, and he was so taken by my mother's dark eyes and slender figure that he went out one morning before daylight and brought her waterlilies that were just opening in the morning sun. She never forgot that, nor, probably, did Bradford.

Unlike Bradford, our sometimes guide Bill was a small, red-faced man of vast understatement. But Bill faithfully tended the boat and helped us keep our poles baited for white perch that ran up to two pounds. Every ten minutes or so, he would reach over the side of the skiff and scoop up water with both hands to smooth back his long gray hair—we never knew if that was vanity or some sort of therapy. But one day, during which he had characteristically said absolutely nothing, he made what was, for him, a significant speech. As we drifted, watching our lines, the cork on his pole plunged so quickly it shot a spurt of water a foot into the air. Instantly, the pole bent sharply until the tip was in the water, levering Bill off the seat. We thought he was going overboard until the pole snapped in two places. Bill held the butt momentarily until the line parted with a loud twang, catapulting him backward into the bottom of the boat like a sack of feed.

We watched in amazement as he regained his seat with great dignity. Methodically, he wet his hair and sat for a long moment looking off nowhere in particular.

"Rockfish," he said finally.

My grandfather's tackle consisted of a split-cane, Heddon casting rod and a Pflueger Supreme bait-casting reel with black linen line and a short length of gut leader. His favorite lures were old wooden plugs, some with glass eyes, all scarred from use—a frog-colored Jitterbug, a Lucky 13, and several Creek Chub crippled minnows, as well as a few Johnson Silver Minnows, Al Foss Shimmy wigglers, and Oriental wigglers that were rigged with pork rind trailers. He especially liked to use a Hawaiian wiggler and pork rind worked along the surface over the weeds in the goose pond. I don't recall that we caught many big bass—a two-pound largemouth was cause for celebration, although I recollect that he once caught two nice rockfish—but perhaps that was because we were almost always vacationing in the hot summer months when fishing for bass and stripers was generally poor.

Some years earlier, Granddad had caught a nine-pound bass, but when he returned with it in the evening, his cronies convinced him that he ought to put it in a wire fish cage that was kept in the water next to the cookshack.

"It'll keep him alive and fresh," they told him.

What they neglected to mention was that there was a hole in the wire that covered the lower end of the cage—a hole large enough, it turned out, for Granddad's trophy to escape.

Granddad often told that tale—he enjoyed a joke on himself—but he had an even greater appreciation for another story involving a shirttail. Lots of these were tacked to the wall behind the woodstove—if you missed a shot at a deer, your hunting companions would cheerfully cut off the tail of your shirt and mount it there as evidence of your poor marksmanship. But this one was special.

"They claimed I had missed a deer," Granddad liked to recount. "I explained that I had shot at a goose, but they didn't believe me. They heard the shot. I didn't have a deer or a goose. Case closed. When we got back to the cabin that evening, they fixed their end-of-the-day drinks as usual and kidded me all through supper about what was going to happen to my shirt."

While they were finishing up the dishes, Granddad slipped away for a few minutes and put on Ted Deloach's shirt—he was the one most bent on upholding this tradition. After supper, Ted made a short, largely insulting speech, wheeled my grandfather around, and cut off the tail of that shirt all the way to the collar. Then he tacked it to the wall and stepped back to admire it.

"How do you think it looks up there?" Ted asked my grandfather.

"Looks fine, Ted, especially since it's not my shirt," said Granddad.

"Well, whose is it then?" Ted asked.

"It's yours, Ted." The shirttail stayed on the wall, and no one loved to tell about it more than Ted Deloach. Except, of course, my grandfather.

Through the years, the little town of Columbia was an eagerly anticipated way-stop, a place to stretch our legs for the final assault. We would stop at the service station just beyond the single-lane bridge (now gone). Sucking on sodas,

we would venture through the village past the old Columbia Hotel (rooms $2–$4) and down side streets. Or we would
walk over to the catfish factory on the banks of the Scuppernong. I swore that one day, if I couldn't live in a cabin
perched a foot over the water three miles beyond Fort Landing, I would live in Columbia. Or in Tyrrell County's second
largest metropolis, Gum Neck, near the Frying Pan. Or in
the big house (also long gone) across from the small store
at Fort Landing, where I would prosper on Zero candy bars
and TruAde. I didn't realize that my summers in this vast
and wondrous place were soon to end. Nor would it have
occurred to me or my friend Charlie Ogletree that he and
his family would settle there years later, he as the county's
only lawyer and his wife Midge as a highly respected school-
teacher. Nor did it seem possible that all those wrecked cars
crudely painted with "Eat at Carley's" advertisements that
sat every few hundred yards on the shoulders of US 64 for
twenty miles on either side of Columbia would someday
be hauled away—or that Carley's Café itself would become
only a memory.

In the early 1950s, I vaguely remember talk that the cabin
was settling and would need expensive repairs—the boathouse, long unused, had already collapsed—but when you
are young and your family is healthy and together, you have
little sense that anything will ever change, especially things
so dear and seemingly permanent.

During those last years, high tides more frequently
flooded the floors of the cabin, so that the decoys would
float out of their piles in the corners, and you sometimes
had to wear boots to get around. But occasional high water
had always been one of the more charming inconveniences.
One night years earlier when water had flooded the cabin,
my grandfather awoke with what he called "an inclination."
As he was fumbling around in the dark looking for his boots,
he made enough noise to wake John Edwards.

"What are you doing, Bullet?" Edwards asked, using the
nickname my grandfather had long held because his head
was as bereft of hair as, well, a bullet.

"I've got to go out a minute," Granddad explained modestly.

"You're going to wade out there in the dark across a flooded narrow boardwalk all the way to the outhouse just to take a leak?" howled Edwards. "For God's sake, why in hell don't you just roll over and let her rip. With this tide, it'll probably beat you back in here anyway."

As my obsession with fishing grew, I came to believe what all fishermen believe—that you can stockpile luck. The theory is that the longer you go without catching a fish, the bigger that fish will be. On one of our later family trips— quite possibly the last in 1955 or 1956—I determined that my time had come to catch a big bass. Granddad's nine-pounder was still out there for all I knew, and I was certainly due. That summer, I still got up before dawn to fish the boardwalks, and I still fished for white perch and sunfish when that was the only option offered, but I had largely retired my first piece of fishing tackle, a paint-cracked green and white cork. I now had a new Shakespeare spinning rod and reel and several lures.

Whenever I could persuade Granddad or the guide, we fished solely for bass. We fished the little cove around the cabin, the goose pond, the shores and upper reaches of the Little Alligator, the shoals in the mouth of the Big Alligator, the Frying Pan, anywhere largemouth bass were likely to be caught. But, of course, it was dead-hot July or August as usual, and the fishing was poor along the shallow shorelines where I was certain bass lurked along grassy edges and among the flooded cypress. Day after day, I cast while others soaked bait. I caught only one bass that my Nip-I-Diddee must have snagged in mid-yawn. It was small—maybe ten inches—but I was sure it was a sign of what was to come.

On the last day, I fished all morning while the dishes were washed and gear was packed and loaded. When it was finally time to leave, I was still walking the boardwalks, casting furiously, retrieving the Nip-I-Diddee so rapidly that it left a wake like a small motorboat. I was certain that my trophy would catch up with it any moment.

They were calling. One more cast, I said. One more. One

more. They were all in the boats. The outboards were running. Finally Dad came and gently led me to the boat.

I saw the cabin once more on a cold January morning in the 1980s. Or rather, I saw where it had been. Arrangements had been made to hunt blinds up the Little Alligator, but we also set aside one day to run down the river and hunt in the goose pond. That day, our guide agreed to swing by the marshy hook just before dawn so I could take a quick look. Even in the dim light, it was apparent that the cabin, cookshack, and outhouse had finally settled beneath the water. Only fishermen knew there was anything left of it.

"We catch a lot of bass there now in warm weather," said the guide. "It's good cover." It would not have occurred to him that I found that highly ironic.

It was a frigid, windless day that didn't yield any ducks, but late that afternoon, luminous clouds wrapped the goose pond in a close, silvery blanket and a brittle snow began to fall. Three swans flew over high, their thin gooselike honking the only sound save the faint tick of snowflakes on the dry bayberry leaves that bushed the blind.

A few weeks later, I called on the last surviving member of my grandfather's original Fort Landing group to tell him about my trip. He was saddened to hear that the cabin was gone.

"We couldn't build a place like that now," he said. "Environmental regulations, you know. Good reasons for them, but something has been lost. I couldn't go anyway with my health like it is, but not many days pass that I don't think about that place. How very lucky, how privileged, we were."

I nodded in agreement.

"I guess my shirttail went down with it, the one I cut off your grandfather's back," he said. "Have you heard that story?"

"Maybe," I replied. "Why don't you tell it to me."

WHEN
FIRST
WE WENT
SPINNING

For saltwater fishermen, the modern era arrived in the 1950s. For me, especially, it arrived in the summer of 1952 on the end of a pier at Long Beach. I was twelve years old.

As was customary each July, Mom and Dad would pack the small trailer and load up my brothers and me for the long, un-air-conditioned trip from Halifax County to spend two weeks in the cottage we always rented. I think Graham and John and I would first begin to see sandy roadsides and smell "salt air" somewhere around Greenville. Hurricane Hazel put an end to our Long Beach vacations in the fall of 1954, and it seems so long ago now that those summers have melted together. Yet they're the kind of memories you can sometimes retrieve in bits and pieces while listening to Billie Holiday alone late at night.

I remember passing the long rows of mothballed Liberty ships pulled up along the lower Cape Fear. I remember the sulfury smell of the treated drinking water, a smell that permeated the cottage even though the windows were always open. There were Mom's lunches of homegrown tomatoes in sugar and vinegar and sliced country ham and early morning family walks to hunt shells. I recall the small, crude sailboats I would make to play with in the surf. And I remember pretty Maxine who, like me, was so shy that she hardly ever spoke to me even though her family always stayed in the cottage across the street the same weeks we were there.

Lest you think me too sentimental, however, I should admit that what I remember best was fishing. I had a True Temper solid glass, five-and-a-half-foot bait-casting rod and a Penn 109 star-drag reel, and when I wasn't fishing the surf with shrimp, I was wheedling Dad to take me to Lockwood's Folly Inlet so I could cast lures for bluefish or speckled trout.

I was also beginning to fish the ocean piers, but their potential wasn't really being tapped yet. For one thing, just about everyone fished with bait using short boat rods made of solid fiberglass or Calcutta cane and revolving-spool Ocean City–type reels with braided lines. Those who could cast without a backlash could get fair distance with several ounces of weight, but many people fished pretty much straight down. Fishing was often good, though, and lots of local farmers and their wives filled tin lard stands with spots and sea mullet that they would salt down or freeze for the winter.

When schools of blues or other game fish passed, fishermen who had longer cane rods and jigging reels would try to cast spoons or Seahawks, and I sometimes managed to catch a few bluefish on my True Temper by casting an abalone spoon on a wire leader behind a two-ounce trolling weight. Even so, casting a light lure any respectable distance was pretty much out of the question.

It soon became apparent that the end of the pier was the place to be if you had higher aspirations. It was here that a plug caster had the best chance of intercepting a school of blues. Also, the end of the pier was where the truly serious big-game fishermen with big Penn Senator reels and stout rods hung out and experimented with tactics for king mackerel, cobia, and tarpon. A live bluefish rigged under a big cork could be free-floated away from the pier, and since there were never more than two or three float fishermen, tangles could be avoided. Fishing was good, and almost every day, there would be strikes from kings.

But for most pier fishermen, it was a matter of soaking bait or sitting and waiting for schools of blues and Spanish that never seemed to get quite close enough. That changed in a hurry.

One day, a man arrived on the end of the pier with a very strange outfit. The rod was much longer than anything we were used to seeing, and it had huge ring guides. The reel hung down under the reel seat on a long metal foot, and the line was this odd-looking clear stuff that looked like some sort of silkworm gut. Monofilament, he called it.

He stood a moment and eyed a school of blues that was feeding off the end of the pier well out of our range. Then he made a cast that seemed to carry forever until his spoon landed with a tiny splash just beyond the school. Instantly, he was hooked up. We watched in astonishment as he caught fish after fish and sauntered off the pier carrying a bucketful. That man, whoever he was, had just sold saltwater spinning outfits to a whole generation of anglers who were on the pier that day. No doubt similar scenarios were being played out up and down the coast around the same time.

You couldn't buy such outfits in local stores at the time. That Christmas, Dad ordered mine from Klein's in Chicago and paid $36 for it—a lot of money back then—and the next summer, I arrived on the pier with my new nine-foot Conolon hollow glass rod and Langley Spinator reel filled with 300 yards of mono. For the first time in my life—maybe the only time—I was on the cutting edge of technology.

I still have that rod and reel. The rod guides and ferrule have been replaced several times and the original finish is long gone, but the reel still works fine, though the drag is not smooth by modern standards. I use that outfit from time to time, and there is no telling how many fish it has caught.

But I never rig it up without thinking of the day nearly fifty years ago when that fisherman heaved a spoon to the horizon and caught a bluefish. Saltwater fishing hasn't been the same since.

SAYING GOOD-BYE TO A LANDMARK

"It was such a strange feeling to drive up to the Emerald Isle Pier," my son Scott told me after he and some friends had made a spring trip to the beach. "I had heard rumors that it might be taken down after Bertha and Fran destroyed most of the pier last summer, but it was still a shock to find so little left. Even the tackle shop and lunch counter were gone. I guess I had hoped that somehow it might be rebuilt."

We talked for a while about memories associated with the pier. Scott has been fishing the pier since the mid-1970s, and I first fished there in 1960 after Mom and Dad built their cottage about two miles west of it. Beach property wasn't in great demand—memories of Hurricane Hazel were still too fresh—and you could take your choice of oceanfront lots for $3,000. Not only were there no other cottages in sight, but there were no cottages whatever for eight miles to the inlet, except right at the Bogue Pier—the two-lane blacktop ended just past Bogue at the ferry slip on the soundside. In fact, except for the tiny village of Salter Path, there wasn't much but beach and maritime forest all the way back to Atlantic Beach.

We walked for miles along deserted beaches, exploring the dunes and shell-scattered washes behind the beach and the untouched maritime forest farther beyond. There was no trash, no sign of man except for the occasional weathered board or old sand-blasted bottle.

But it was on the Emerald Isle Pier that I spent most of my time in my late teens and early twenties. In those early years when Earl Thompson owned it, it was a steel girder pier.

In more recent years, after it had been nibbled by various storms, it was considerably shorter and most of the steel had been replaced by wood pilings. Fishermen came over from Cape Carteret by the ferry or, more likely, drove out from Atlantic Beach. Except for the rustic Emerald Isle Motel (replaced by condos some years ago), there was nowhere to stay, and many people slept in their trucks or rented one of the trailers clustered at the pier.

You could find the same people fishing the pier every trip, and all of them became part of a vast, extended family. Fairly early on, Ken Heverly and his wife bought the pier, and through the 1960s, 1970s, and 1980s, we all watched our kids grow up while we float fished for king mackerel off the end, plugged for blues and Spanish, or fished inshore for flounder, pompano, spots, sea mullet, and other species. Fishing was good, and the only time the pier was truly crowded was in the fall when the weather was crisp and the schools of bait were heading south. You came to know that certain look when the autumn water had a brisk green chop and bait glittered underneath. You knew fishing would be peak for just about everything worth catching, and farm families would bring buckets and fill them with spots. Scott, my brother John, and I would often fish on the pier from dawn to dark for a week or more, losing all track of time.

Although the fishing has been poor in recent years and some old friends are long gone, lots of people are going to miss this place.

"It was the first stop on nearly every trip, sometimes even before we bothered to unload the car," Scott recalled. "Couldn't wait to find out what was biting. I caught my first Spanish mackerel and bluefish on plugs there when I was very small. I loved to drag minnows or stripbait around the pilings for flounder. Something interesting was always happening. It seems only a year or so ago that I hooked a king on a plug and lost it around the pilings.

"I still catch myself thinking I can go up and plug for an hour or two for Spanish mackerel after supper as I always did. Or go buy a hamburger and a drink and just hang around and talk to someone while they watch their rods.

There are other piers, of course, but it won't ever be the same."

"You know," Scott added. "I noticed that the sign for the pier was still out at the road. I had my picture taken standing under it."

WHERE
ARE
YOU,
RALPH?

The second thing you notice is that no one is talking anymore. The predawn joviality at the dock begins to peter out just about the time you pass the sea buoy. A solemn, almost ominous, stillness settles on the anglers as they become entranced by the foamy wake and the rhythmic roar of the diesels. One would think this is a particularly reflective group of fishermen, quietly appreciating the raw power of the open sea. It is a bit less than that.

This unlikely moment of dignity is the result of the first thing you noticed as the boat began to pick up the roll of the sea—that there was a funny little acrid taste in the back of your mouth somewhere along the base of the tongue, and your throat seemed to be ever-so-slightly swollen. Well, you thought, the joke I was about to tell will keep. Just getting my sea legs, you know. I'll be fine. Is Portugal really out there? How fascinating.

I know this brand of hearty optimism very well. You can set your watch by what will happen to me next. Within three minutes, I will have bolted for the lee gunnel and be tossing groceries to the four winds. And isn't it precious beyond all words how those who are seldom afflicted describe the experience? We are said to be "barfing," "hurling," "calling Ralph," "tossing our cookies," "blowing lunch," and, my favorite, "chumming."

I envy those who never get seasick. My ruling passions are old ships, the wine-dark sea, and fishing, and yet I invariably get sick half a mile off the beach. Some sea captain I would make—Patrick O'Brien's hero Jack Aubrey would cut me adrift if I sullied one of the holystoned decks of his frigate, the HMS *Surprise*. Since I was ten years old, I have built wooden model sailing ships, but if I so much as hold a twenty-inch brig in front me and give it a bit of a rocking motion, I get cross-eyed.

No problem, you say. Just take a seasickness remedy. Try Dramamine, Dramamine II, Marezin, or one of the newer prescription patches you stick behind your ear. Fine, except the only ones that work for me also put me to sleep. I once took Dramamine an hour or so before we were to go off-shore. Because of heavy seas, the captain called off our trip at the last minute, so we went to the inlet to fish. I passed out for hours on the hot sand in 95-degree heat. The circling buzzards woke me at dusk.

On a trip this past summer, I thought I had found the answer in some of these newer remedies that are not supposed to make you sleepy. Indeed, we'd gotten almost all the way to the Gulf Stream and I was feeling wide awake and cocky until I realized that I needed to tie an Albright special before I would be ready to fish for dolphin with flies. By the time I'd finished tying that knot, I knew I would shortly have an opportunity to enjoy my breakfast yet again.

Of course, most people can do some things to forestall or lessen the effects of seasickness, although they haven't worked all that well for me. First, by all means take medication in advance. Your pharmacist or doctor can make recommendations, and you'll need a prescription for the patches anyway. Seasickness remedies work very well for most people, but I would try to avoid those that warn of drowsiness—why pay $600 for an offshore nap?

A few other tips may help. Stay in the open air, chew gum, and watch the horizon if you feel queasy. Don't go below, where the stench of toilet chemicals will surely do you in. Also, avoid standing just above the diesel exhaust. There are two schools of thought on eating: some say eat a light breakfast, while others suggest hearty fare on the theory that it at least gives you some ammunition. I'm not prepared to make specific recommendations, but perhaps you will recall what the ever-thoughtful Tweety-bird offered Sylvester when the latter was in the early throes of mal de mer. "Here, Puddy," said Tweety. "You look like you could use a nice piece of greasy pork."

The one bout of seasickness I remember above all others took place out of Morehead City over thirty years ago on an old converted PT boat named the *Danco.* I had worked that summer to save money for a head boat trip, and sick or not, I was determined to fish. Indeed, I was doing fairly well until I mistook my box lunch for some ripe squid (the sandwiches and bait were passed out in identical paper cartons). I barely made it to the rail, where I managed to throw up right into the gaping maw of a very nice red snapper that another fisherman had just winched to the surface.

The angler was livid and refused to bring the fish aboard. Instead, he cut his line and stalked off to try his luck from another spot along the rail.

I was too sick to enjoy this at the time, but I recall thinking that he could have rinsed off that snapper. Besides, I would have swapped him a brace of untainted black sea bass for it. After all, it isn't often you catch the main course and the stuffing at the same time.

A PAIR
OF DUCKS
IS NO
PARADOX

When the pair of mallards showed up on the pond behind my cabin early last spring, my first thought was that they might be wild ducks that were nesting somewhere nearby. But they were too tame, and a closer look revealed that they were domestic hybrids—Merita ducks, my kids call them. We didn't feed them any white bread, and whenever I went fishing, they would simply swim to the other side of the pond and watch. I wondered how they'd gotten there, but it wasn't until sometime later that I finally got around to asking Curtis about them. Curtis does the actual farming hereabouts, while I pay some bills and try not to get in the way.

"Melvin brought them over and turned them loose," Curtis explained. "You know Melvin; he helps me sometimes. You don't mind, do you?"

"Oh no, they're fine," I said. "I've gotten sort of attached to them. A pond needs ducks like a yard needs concrete chickens."

For the next month or so, I saw the mallards—a drake and a hen—every time I went to the farm. When the hen disappeared, I began to wonder if some little ducklings might not soon be joining us. But no ducklings appeared, nor did the hen return.

Even though I fished the pond for only a few hours every week or so, the drake was always there. Usually I would find him sitting on the protruding stump of a willow tree that had fallen over into the pond near the dam. He no longer swam very much, and I made the common anthropomorphic mistake of assuming that he was despondent. And yes,

I'd sometimes carry on the kind of one-sided conversation that is part of our arrogant need to humanize all things.

"What's the matter, old boy?" I'd ask. "Am I invading your space, or are you still pining for your sweetheart? I'll move on as soon as I make a few casts here."

By mid-July, the drake had become a permanent stump potato. I could understand what might pass for loneliness in a duck, even brief bereavement, but there was no obvious biological explanation for this duck's behavior. After all, almost all wild creatures—and certainly ducks—are notoriously opportunistic when it comes to relationships. Even the popular notion that geese are monogamous throughout their lives is nonsense. The morals of your average Canada, male or female, would make tabloid headlines. So what was bugging this duck?

One afternoon late in August, I slid my twelve-foot john-boat into the pond to fish an hour or so before dark. As usual, the drake was on his stump. I had been fishing about twenty minutes when I heard splashing and saw that the duck was in the water beside the stump, flapping its wings. I have seen ducks do that frequently, possibly just to stretch.

"Well, my friend, it's good to see you getting back to normal," I said, and I made another cast. A minute or two passed before it dawned on me that the duck was still splashing. I stopped fishing and began to watch. Something wasn't quite right. The drake seemed to be trying to fly, but he was very low in the water. And why was he moving backward? Suddenly, I knew what this duck had known all along about missing mates and the safety of stumps.

I threw my rod into the bottom of the boat and jammed the electric motor into high gear. The duck disappeared just as I arrived at the spot, but by reaching into the water as deeply as possible, I managed to grab him by the neck. I could feel the weight of something big, then the weight was gone and I pulled the duck into the boat. One rear leg was torn from the socket, and the thigh was raw meat.

I never saw the snapping turtle. The duck sat dazed in the bottom of the boat while I pondered what to do. It could not survive; indeed, I had only prolonged its suffering. Clearly, my interference was the only element out of place. I could wring its neck, but even that act of presumed mercy would reflect the kind of contrived sentiment that has led humans to a profound misunderstanding of the relationship between predator and prey. We are all one or the other—some of us both—and nothing about that arrangement is cruel or immoral. Nature, for all its grace and beauty, is relentlessly unsentimental, has no regard whatever for the individual and arguably reduces even compassion to an instinct.

I picked up the dying duck and placed it gently in the water. If you feel you must say good-bye to a duck—and I did—you should at least recognize that it makes just as much sense to apologize to a snapping turtle for interrupting its meal.

I turned the boat around and headed back to the dam. When I looked back, the duck was gone. I caught a nice bass next to the stump and turned it loose. I don't much care for the taste of fish and release them because I might catch them again someday. Like the snapper, had I been hungry, I would have kept the duck.

DRESSED
TO KILL

I had a vague sense of apprehension the minute I spotted the advertisement. A stunning woman with immaculate blond hair was standing knee-deep in a salt marsh. She was holding a clam rake in an unfamiliar manner, the way Mother Teresa might hold, say, an assault rifle. The young lady's smile seemed a bit forced, too, no doubt because she had been out there in the hot sun posing among mosquitoes and deerflies for a long time. Obviously, she had also observed that salt marshes do not smell quite as good as your average lawn.

It was what she was wearing, however, that gave me hives. She had on a pink, button-down cotton shirt and plaid Bermuda shorts. Draped casually over her shoulders was a lime green sweater with the sleeves looped into a lazy knot across the front. Somebody had shod her with a pair of hip boots rolled down the way a Harkers Island loon hunter might wear them, except they were uncommonly clean. Somehow, you sensed that an assistant was standing close by with a garden hose and a twenty-five-gallon drum of bug spray. The title of the photo was "Muffy goes clamming," but Muffy didn't look all that enthused about this new direction in fashion.

This was about ten years ago, as I recall, and now we all know where Muffy was headed. Within a few years, *Vogue, Glamour, GQ,* and other fashion literati were hyping the raw, primitive look that had so long been the dominion of nomads, hunters, arctic explorers, fishermen, bird dog trainers, and various other old coots and unrepentant originals. Now we've got ersatz cowboys like Calvin Klein skipping around New York City in predistressed denim jackets and jeans (he couldn't distress his own, for heaven sakes?). Polo is marketing hunting shirts (just the thing to wear to an animal rights demonstration). Venerable Abercrombie and Fitch went bankrupt and was reborn as a preppie haberdashery more likely to sell you a tie rack than a gun rack.

You can even see the changes in the catalogs of such longtime outdoor suppliers as Eddie Bauer and L. L. Bean. Bean still carries high-quality hunting and fishing stuff, including those wonderful rubber-bottomed hunting boots, but these days you're just as likely to see those boots in a gourmet coffee shop as in a thicket of briers and honeysuckle. Indeed, if it weren't for the ads for scented dog beds, some modern sporting catalogs might not look all that much different from Victoria's Secret.

We strike back where we can, of course. One friend of mine recently encountered an acquaintance at a board meeting wearing ostrich-skin cowboy boots with sterling silver toes. Sensing a rare opportunity, he sidled up and asked, "Do you know the difference between a real cowboy and a fake cowboy?" "Why, no," came the reply. "Real cowboys have the manure on the outside of their boots."

Yet despite scoring an occasional hit, we've clearly lost the war. City streets are full of candy-colored, four-wheel-drive vehicles that have never been off the pavement and are carrying drivers on grocery safaris or bankers dressed as though they were going on a moose hunt during their lunch hour. Briefcases and purses have been replaced by fishing vests and backpacks. What's next—holsters for hair dryers or blaze-orange bustiers and tree bark camo stockings?

This phenomenon has been explained as a secret desire to get in touch with our "inner hairy person" and rediscover the vanishing wilderness. Presumably, this is the same wilderness we have been so diligently paving over. Others say it's also an expression of individuality, but perhaps you have noticed that nonconformists always dress alike (remember the tie-dyed T-shirts of the 1960s?).

All I know is that this trend doesn't seem to have had much impact on those who actually spend any considerable amount of time outdoors. Much to his wife's dismay, a cer-

tain senior member of our family still wears the same thread-
bare, zipper-sprung hunting pants he bought shortly after
high school. Because most of the belt loops are long gone
and his waist is a bit thicker, the pants are held together by
a piece of tobacco twine (pay attention, Calvin!). His favorite old flannel shirt—worn buttoned at the neck—was one-
third of a "three for $5" special purchased around 1950.
His hat is a feed store freebie, his shell vest belonged to his
father, and his boots are Cloverine Salve premiums.

The fact is that real outdoorsmen buy clothes only once
in their lifetime, and then only if they haven't been fortunate enough to inherit them. Clearly, this group does not
constitute a vast pool of potential sales, so I suppose it is
natural for outdoor clothiers to expand into other markets.
But you have to wonder what wilderness experience is re-
captured in a $220 mauve hunting jacket or, for that matter,
a camouflage bikini.

FISHING
CARS
AND
HUNTING
TRUCKS

When I was sixteen years old, I managed to get a stringer of bluegills tangled in the rear wheel spokes of my bicycle. I was tooling along at about ten miles an hour balancing a rod and reel on the handlebars while holding a small metal tackle box in one hand and the stringer in the other. When I regained my senses, the bike and I were facing the direction we had come from, and I was stretched out on the sidewalk looking at skid marks and a trail of mangled sunfish.

Long before the scabs came off, I reached the conclusion that I was going to be seriously handicapped as a global sportsman without a more reliable and spacious mode of transportation. I had seen my deliverance at a used car lot downtown.

"Fishing Car, $35," said the sign tucked under the windshield wiper of a 1940s vintage black sedan—a Ford, I think. I was too young to realize that this was car-lot Latin for "caveat emptor" or that it was commonly applied to any vehicle that was one owner shy of spending the rest of its existence on cinder blocks behind a barn. I didn't know about rolled-back odometers or sawdust in transmissions. Indeed, I hardly noticed the slack tires, the broken window, the wildcat-ravaged upholstery, or the knee-high grass that had grown up around my prize. Rather, I was calculating how long it would take to save that kind of money on a $1-a-week allowance, including birthday and Christmas windfalls. Even so, it was immediately clear to me that no serious angler would ever be complete without four wheels, and I visualized that old jalopy as a sort of rolling tackle box, a ticket to distant adventure.

The salesman finally got the car started with jumper cables, and I can still see the thick cloud of blue smoke that billowed over that end of town. "Don't let that bother you, son," said the salesman. "It's old enough to smoke."

As it turned out, I was in my thirties before I managed to acquire a true fishing and hunting vehicle—that is, a car or truck specifically rigged for sporting purposes. In some respects, that proved to be too soon, considering that it was a 1970 Maverick with 148,000 miles on it. Ah, but that seedy piece of Detroit steel had character, and it became the first of several rolling tackle boxes and gun cabinets I've owned. I've loved every one of them.

Every serious hunter and fisherman dreams of owning a sporting vehicle because it personifies pure freedom. Indeed, the fully realized unit—packed full of tackle, guns, dogs, clothes, food, and camping supplies—contains more life-support systems than a space shuttle. I have always suspected that Izaak Walton—had he lived in this century —would have gladly swapped his pastoral walks to sylvan streams for a chance to drive there in an old pickup. And I don't doubt that he'd tow a boat hung with an outboard powerful enough to plane a coal barge.

"When I get in my old truck, I want to know that I can run an errand downtown or keep going all the way to Alaska," a friend confided. "And some days it don't make a whole lot of difference which it is."

That carefree sentiment surely inhabits the soul of everyone who has owned an old sporting vehicle, and my Maverick fit the tradition. My kids named it Ralph, and at one time, we gave serious consideration to adding red and blue spots to its dark green flanks and red, white, and black fins behind the wheel wells so that it would resemble a brook trout. I never got around to the *Salvelinus fontinalis* paint job, but that was one of the few whims unfulfilled during the nearly ten years I owned that car. It carried me over countless logging roads to remote trout streams in the Southern Appalachians. Together, we chased bass and panfish in dozens of ponds, lakes, and rivers. Bristling with surf rods, Ralph and I prowled the autumn beaches.

On one memorable trip to the Little Tennessee River just before the waters impounded what may have been the best trout stream east of the Mississippi, Ralph and I were surrounded by a contingent of Hell's Angels that decided to share our campsite. Though I was at first apprehensive, my fears proved unfounded. That evening after I finished fishing, the bikers shared my beers and we had a grand time trading tales of conquest—mine were of fishing; theirs were of, well, conquest. I have no doubt that Ralph was the ticket that gained me entrance as a genuine social outcast.

Ralph also took me on my first trip to the limestone valleys of Pennsylvania—a weeklong indulgence of wonderfully picky trout, blizzards of green drakes and sulfurs, and rolling countryside laced with jade-colored streams. We poked around in towns that had the look of pure Americana and traveled back roads between streams listening to Beethoven's piano concertos, Ella Fitzgerald, and Johnny Hartman. What more can you ask of a companion than that you share identical tastes?

Such vehicles are expressions of their owners' personalities. Some are models of efficiency, every item carefully stored. Others more closely resemble the open rear of a city trash compactor, except the gear has been more fully compacted. Certainly Ralph's appearance of shabby utility would have made my great uncle feel right at home. As a child, I spent a good bit of time fishing with him out of his ancient Chevy. I suspect that car had accumulated its 100,000-plus miles without ever leaving the farm or getting out of first gear. It had surely never been washed, and from the driver's window to the rear bumper, the paint was completely eroded by tobacco juice. In addition to a permanent consignment of cane poles sticking out of a rear window, my uncle kept a flourishing worm bed on the floorboard behind the front seat and nourished it regularly like compost with crumbled nabs, Moon Pie wrappers, and well-gnawed toe joints from pickled pigs' feet.

Not all sporting vehicles stay in first gear or move with the stately swiftness of a ring-shot Maverick. Back when he was a young pup, Jack Avent crammed a 312-cubic-inch 1957 Thunderbird mill with three two-barrels into his 1956 Ford truck and painted flames under the hood. It's still hauling us to old millponds and black-water rivers, and it would do so very quickly if we were ever in any hurry. In recent years, he has rigged a large aerated tank in the back to carry big shiners, but it's still a handsome fishing chariot, and surely unique.

More typical is the well-used International Scout Mike Gaddis bought some years ago. It has carried us and an assortment of dogs on many fine hunts, and the engine is still strong, although rumor has it that Mike has been seen buying rust preventive in fifty-gallon drums. I hope that's enough to do the trick because that old four-wheeler is family.

When Ralph's drinking problem reached the stage that I was buying oil by the six-pack, I reluctantly hung a "Fishing Car for Sale" sign on him. Not wanting to take unfair advantage of a fellow angler, I explained the nature of Ralph's addiction and watched an eager youngster drive him off to detox. As it happened, my friend Reid Bahnson was looking for a home for his well-used but carefully maintained 1977 Ford Bronco, a trout-fishing truck that already knew every mountain road and creek in the Appalachians. It's out in the yard now, aging like fine wine and waiting for our next adventure. It will climb anything it can set four feet on, and it's an insult to the neighborhood—both highly desirable qualities.

Eventually, of course, there is always a grim appointment with the junkyard and crusher. Some of my friends, alas, no longer seem to have the energy to nurse a sporting conveyance through advancing stages of decrepitude and have abandoned the geriatric rattletraps of their youth for newer vehicles, some brand new. Just the other day, a bright red truck with the sticker still in the window pulled into my drive.

"Looky here," said its proud owner. "It's got a fancy AM-FM stereo with CD and cassette, king cab, spotlights, built-in dog boxes, four-wheel drive with all-terrain tires, and both heat and air-conditioning. There's enough power under here to pull the battleship *North Carolina* up a steep ramp," he added, patting the hood.

"What say we load it up and take it to the farm this weekend," I suggested. "We could drive across the creek bottom and turn the dogs loose in the swamp field near the sawmill. I haven't been back in there since I got the tractor stuck last summer."

"No way, buddy-ro," he said, wiping a minuscule bird dropping off a fender. "Might get some mud on it."

A
T'ANGLING
WE GO

I have not researched the origins of the word "angle" beyond *Webster's Unabridged Dictionary,* but the various defini-
tions found there are not wholly satisfactory. The angle is
the fishhook, with or without the line and rod (archaic), but
the meaning has also expanded beyond the gear to the act
of fishing—though the dictionary footnotes this usage as
rare. Daniel Webster, himself an obsessive angler, would no
doubt have found that amusing.

I can't prove it, but I am highly suspicious that the word
"tangle" is little more than a corruption of "to angle." The
evidence is purely anecdotal, but you don't have to angle
more than a few minutes to experience an anecdote. Regardless of the mode of fishing I choose, I seem to remain
in a more or less continuous state of entanglement. A cast
that does not wind up in some tree, stump, or bush (complete with an active wasp nest) is very likely to intercept a
submerged limb, lily pad, gob of green algae, or another
fisherman's abandoned line before I have managed to retrieve it. It is a source of wonderment that the various hooks
and lures I use are ever unencumbered long enough to perform their intended tasks. Am I alone here? I think not.

One of our oldest forms of angling is fly fishing, pre-
dating bait casting by several hundred years, likely far
longer, and preceding spinning by another seventy-five or
so. The modern fly rod is a wondrous piece of equipment;
in theory, at least, it is capable of casting a fly a hundred
feet or more. Yet there I was on a bright, windy afternoon
this past spring trying to make a cast half that distance to a

spot where I had seen a very large spawning bass swirl in a shallow pocket against the shoreline.

With the windblown boat spinning on its anchor rope—and me spinning on the seat in the opposite direction in an effort to face the target—I made half a dozen fruitless attempts to place a bug over that bass.

An earlier cast had been carried into a tree two dozen feet down the bank by a sudden gust, another had snared the hook in a guide and tightly twirled thirty feet of line and leader around the rod. My last had left me nesting in loose coils of line with the bug stuck in the back of my shirt. After I cut the bug out of my shirt and redressed, I noticed that I had four hopeless windknots in my leader. "To hell with fly fishing," I said. (I am pretty sure a similar sentiment led early Kentucky watchmakers to craft the first revolving-spool bait-casting reels.)

Still determined to present some enticement to that bass, I picked up a casting rod that had already been rigged with a soft plastic salamander. I should have made a practice cast into open water to clear the line and reacquaint myself with the peculiarities of revolving-spool reels. This is always a good idea anytime you switch tackle, but I was impatient. My cast would have been perfect had I not experienced what is optimistically called a professional overrun. The salamander shot toward the target, stopped abruptly at the zenith of its arc, and plummeted like a gut-shot cormorant. I picked fretfully at the loose loops of line on the spool until the reel was barely visible. History does not record the first occurrence of a backlash, but my guess is that it took place in the last century simultaneously with the watchmakers' first test of their new invention. I began to cut line until fifty yards lay around my feet in short hanks like hair around a barber's chair, then I realized there wasn't enough good line left on the reel to reach the bass. "To hell with bait casting," I said. (Was a vexed Frenchman likewise encouraged to invent the first spinning reel?)

I spotted another vigorous swirl next to the bank. That bass was hot for trouble. I picked up Europe's contribution to angling and fired a cast. The plastic worm sailed straight and true but began to falter as an unnoticed loop on the perimeter of the spinning reel leaped off and dragged a wad of twisted monofilament through the guides with a dry flutter that sounded like a dozen dragonflies mating in a paper sack. The worm fell short. Bunched at the third guide was what appeared to be a large silvery wig. If you think we carry knives to clean fish, think again.

It is a miracle that anyone has the patience to fish, much less that they become absorbed in it enough to do so more than once. Would you not think, with the energies and intellects of countless anglers more or less constantly engaged all this time, that we would have made some noticeable advance in developing tackle and attendant skills that resist such tangles?

Perhaps this is why the truly contented fishermen I know use nothing more elaborate than a cane pole, cork, split shot, and hook. I would do so myself, but I can't figure out how to connect all those components without using line.

BUZZARDS,
BASS,
AND BULL

"Whew, that is intense," I said as Matt Hodgson and I maneuvered my twelve-foot johnboat into position to fish along the dam in one of the ponds at the farm this past summer. I'd caught the first whiff of rotting flesh while we were rigging up our fly rods at the truck, but now that we had crossed the pond, we were directly downwind and obviously much nearer the source.

"Indeed, that's an understatement," said Matt as he wiped his eyes in the late afternoon heat.

"We could load up and go to another pond," I ventured. It was a motion that would have surely passed unanimously had it not been for the fact that sizable largemouths had intercepted our deer-hair bugs on our first casts. The evening's fishing was off to an encouraging start, a welcome change from two near-fishless trips earlier that month. Then a truly nauseating wave arrived on the breeze just as we released those fish. The stench was thick enough to hold a fork upright.

As we gasped for breath, there was a sudden clatter in the woods just behind the dam. A dozen vultures, alarmed at our presence, abandoned their repast and flapped heavily into the limbs of a tall pine. So gorged were they with carrion that several broke the stout, living branches they had chosen and fell thirty feet to the ground like sacks of feed. Another sticky wave of rot—so vaporous it was nearly visible—rolled over us.

"It must be one of the two bulls that got out of the pasture a few weeks ago and has been running wild," I said. "Curtis caught one but not the other."

"You sure he caught one?" gagged Matt. "I would have no problem believing both bulls—indeed, his entire herd—had met with misfortune."

There was but one choice, and it didn't need further discussion. While satiated buzzards fell out of trees and the rest squabbled over their malodorous meal, we cast through the viscous atmosphere. It was clearly suppertime, above and below, a time ripe for scavengers of every ilk to seize the moment. We caught a dozen fat largemouths. That may well have been last season's most memorable day of bass bugging—bull and buzzards notwithstanding.

The truth is that fish simply don't go on wild feeding sprees all that often, and you can't waste an opportunity. Even if you fish a lot, you may not encounter such conditions more than a few times a year. Sure, there are trips when ideal weather, handsome surroundings, and other serendipitous contributions mark a day as special, but it helps amazingly if the fish cooperate.

"You would quickly get bored with fishing if the fish practically leaped into the boat every time you went," a companion once told me. "It would be no challenge." This observation, by the way, comes from a companion who never fails to note that "it is good just getting out" following any trip when our execution has fallen short of our hopes. Alas, it has been "good just getting out" far too often to suit me.

Yet once in a rare while, fishermen are rewarded for their persistence even when the odds seem to be against it. It was 95-plus at four o'clock one afternoon later this past summer when Jack Avent and I launched the boat in a pond. Given the conditions, we had no unrealistic expectations.

Two hours later, we had a five-gallon bucket full of big crappies and bluegills that we'd caught on ultralight spinning tackle using jigs. As the shadows stretched across the pond, we sat the bucket on the bank and rigged our fly rods. In the sultry stillness after sundown, bass sucked in our floating deer-hair bugs on nearly every cast—two bass weighed nearly four pounds—and we wound up catching at least fifteen. Did it bother us that our skills were not challenged? Not a bit. Every fisherman deserves a day like that occasionally. For one thing, it reminds us how unsatisfying, by comparison, it is to have poor luck and lie about it. Dangerous too.

Some years ago, my son Scott and daughter Susan accompanied me on a trip out West to fish for wild browns and rainbows. We didn't have a guide the first afternoon we arrived, but we were eager to get started and spent a few hours fishing a short stretch of the upper Madison River. Later, back at camp, we ran into two other fishermen. "Any luck?" I asked.

"We smoked 'em big time," they said enthusiastically. "Must have caught two dozen nice rainbows and a few browns up to nineteen inches. How did you do?"

I allowed that we had not done quite so well. I was content to leave it at that, but Susan wasn't.

"We smoked two little ones," she added cheerfully.

FINISHING
TOUCHES

By the time I'd picked up supplies at Southern States and stopped to get gas, the boat I was towing was beginning to attract attention. A twelve-foot aluminum johnboat makes a pretty good trailer if the load isn't too heavy, and it was piled up with bales of hay, bags of fertilizer, a herbicide sprayer, and a lawn mower and gas can. Several cane poles were tied on top with tobacco twine. My old 1977 Bronco was filled halfway up the windows with its usual load of fishing tackle, nets, paddles, trolling motors, batteries, toolboxes, spare clothing, and other more or less permanent accessories. During the warm months, I use the Bronco as a sort of rolling tackle box. Beginning in late fall, it undergoes a monthlong conversion into a mobile mud room, gun cabinet, decoy bag, and dog cage.

"You working, fishing, or are you gonna be in a *Grapes of Wrath* reenactment?" asked the station attendant.

"Nah, I'm heading for the farm," I said. "I doubt I'll have time to fish this trip. Too much work to do. I don't think I'll ever be finished." (I say things like that because it sounds so much better than the truth, which is that I can usually find time to fish. Whether I will also find time to do any actual work is more often what is in doubt.)

But this trip, I had chores that took precedence, and it didn't appear too likely that I would have time to dawdle, not that there weren't temptations. Ripe blackberries and plums bordered the dirt path as I drove past fields of chest-high tobacco. The clean rows were in perfect condition for an hour or two of arrowhead hunting, and the dark water in the ponds looked especially inviting. I could see ripples where a large bass moved along the edge of a bed of lily pads. It was an ideal place to pitch a plastic worm. Maybe later, I thought.

In the 93-degree afternoon heat, I spread hay around the young fruit trees, then placed bales in a ditch that was threatening to erode the edge of a field. The next two hours were spent spraying the poison ivy, cow itch, and Virginia creeper that were covering the sides of pack houses and tobacco barns. Then I fertilized two of the ponds and mowed around the old three-room tenant house that I had converted into a rough fishing and hunting cabin a few years earlier. I stopped to tack up several loose boards and repaired a step. By the time I finished, it was getting late. One of these days, I thought, if I ever finish this place, I'm going to settle down and enjoy it.

On the back porch of the cabin, I poured a tub of water and washed off the hay, fertilizer, and grime, then sat wearily in an old rocker and watched the sun set. Lightning bugs glittered across the fields, and a bobwhite gave a few last sleepy calls just as the toads and bullfrogs began to get cranked up. It was time to go. But I didn't. Instead, I walked into the cabin and rummaged through the Hoosier to see if I could find a snack to hold me until I reached civilization and a fast-food joint.

Hmmm, I'd forgotten about that bag of cornmeal, and here was a jar of vinegar, which reminded me of the tomatoes and cucumbers I'd picked earlier. Maybe I should eat here. There was milk in a cooler in the truck. Maybe, it suddenly occurred to me, I should simply spend the night. Why not? What was the rush, anyway? What, really, is ever the rush? There were beds in the cabin and a pile of old magazines to read. I didn't have a bathroom or electricity, but I'd solved those problems by adding porches (think of them as half baths), oil lamps, and a Home Comfort wood cookstove. Besides, if I got up early, I could pay a visit to that bass in the lily pads.

Supper was a pan of corn bread cooked on the woodstove, sliced tomatoes and cucumbers in vinegar and pepper, and a quart of cold milk. I read an ancient *Reader's Digest* by oil light until bedtime—the big news was polio and the threat of low-flying nuclear bombers—then on an impulse I took a walk up the path through the farm past the orchard. The moon was nearly full except for a bite out of one corner. It was so bright I could see ants crawling on the path, and the humidity gave the air a hazy, luminous quality.

I sat on the crest of a hill for a long time with the farm spread out around me like a silvery blanket. Tucked into a distant fold was the faint glow of a lamp in the window of the cabin. Looking at that square of warm light, I realized that this must have been what I had in mind when I first began to fix it up. So what if it never got finished—it looked finished from here. Maybe cabins, like life, are works in progress.

FISHING'S FOURTH LEVEL

Several years ago, a very nice family from Mexico moved to our farm to help Curtis and Louise with the planting, harvest, and other seemingly endless chores. The boys have been going to school here, and they speak English so well that they often serve as translators for their parents, Curtis, Louise, and me since we're all past that age when learning a new language is easy. But we have no problems, except I'm astonished they don't laugh harder when they hear me fracture a Spanish phrase.

I would reckon Isidro Jr. to be about fifteen. Late last summer, he was learning how to drive on the dirt paths around the farm, and he would wave at me whenever he passed the little three-room house I use as a getaway. One afternoon, he and three of his friends bounced to a stop in his dusty Chevette and asked if it would be all right if they fished in the pasture pond.

"Sure," I replied. "Bring a bucket and keep all the bluegills, crappies, and other panfish you catch. Just turn loose the bass because they help keep the pond in balance."

They were back in a few minutes with their gear. I had work to do so I didn't join them, but they were still fishing in the late afternoon when I finished up and walked down to the pond to see how they were doing. They had not caught a single fish.

"No bites?" I asked incredulously. "Nothing?"

"No bites," Isidro said, shrugging. "But we are having fun. I think I almost had a bite once."

That was when I noticed their tackle. Except for an old push-button spinning outfit, they had only weathered cane poles or sticks cut in the woods. A glass jar containing half a dozen big grasshoppers lay nearby in the grass. They had neither red worms nor crickets. I looked at the terminal rigs on the poles—most were baited with very large grass- hoppers on hooks big enough for king mackerel, and there were no split shot for weight under the corks. One fisher- man had simply been dangling a plastic grub motionless in the water.

"What's on the spinning rod?" I asked, looking out to- ward the middle of the pond, where I could see a cork the size of a softball. The fisherman reeled it in. "What do you think?" he asked.

Hanging a foot beneath the cork was a Little George— a lead-head lure with a rear-mounted Colorado blade. Con- sidering that it's designed mostly for distance casting for schooling fish on big lakes, it would be hard to imagine a more inappropriate choice. Impaled on its large treble hook were three giant grasshoppers.

"Holy smoke, guys," I said, or something like that. "I be- lieve I see your problem. Tell you what, you go over there in the shade behind that tobacco barn where the dirt is soft and moist and dig some worms while I see if I can find some hooks and stuff in my truck."

In a few minutes, I had rigged their gear with smaller hooks and split shot, and I showed them how to bait the hooks, hiding the points in the bodies of the worms. "Adjust the corks so that you're fishing on or very near the bottom," I explained.

Almost immediately, they began to catch bluegills. It didn't matter that the fish were small. Laughing and shout- ing, they hauled them in as fast as they could bait their hooks. They were still at it when I had to leave, but they all stopped to wave. I had not thought to ask, but I don't think any of them had ever caught a fish before.

During the forty-five-minute drive home, it occurred to me that I had been given the answer to something that had puzzled me for years. When I was ten years old and just learning to fish, I was never able to understand why my grandfather took such obvious pleasure in watching me catch fish. Invariably, he made sure that I caught something, frequently sacrificing his own opportunities to do so. Even when I was older and more experienced, he would still position the boat to give me the first cast to any spot that was likely to yield a bass. I hadn't understood that then, but it was clear enough now.

There's an old saying that fishermen go through three stages of evolution. In the beginning, they try to see how many fish they can catch. Then they concentrate on catching the biggest fish. Finally, they seek only the most difficult fish. But I suspect there must be another, more subtle level at which the most satisfying fish is the one you help someone else catch.

I wouldn't claim my evolution is complete, but thanks to Isidro and his friends, I'm getting there.

COUNTRY
STORE
GOURMET

Rare is the hunter or fisherman who can accurately be called a gourmet. Most of us think that Chateaubriand for two is a love nest in a shabby French hotel or that aspic is something you wear around your neck.

And yet the outdoorsman has a very special—some would say unusual—appreciation for food that inevitably manifests itself away from home. For example, I cannot eat a tomato from my backyard garden unless I first pick out all the seeds, and the only green vegetable I like is key lime pie. But let me spot a raw, dirt-stained turnip in a field while I'm bird hunting, and I'll wipe it on my pants and devour it with gusto. If I'm on a wilderness trout stream, happiness is a couple of liverwurst and onion sandwiches mashed into a lump in the back of my vest. Would I eat that at home? Would you? Indeed, I might turn up my nose at a water-spotted wine glass at home, but I'll drink contentedly from a woodland spring clogged with dead leaves and live salamanders.

Why is that? Who knows really. It seems that food and drink just taste better out there, and no doubt you—like me—have fond memories of such things as oysters roasted on a November beach or peach cobbler cooked in a Dutch oven buried in the embers of a dying campfire. Or maybe it's venison tenderloins simmered in butter and sour cream in a Downeast deer camp or mountainous breakfasts served at 4:30 in the morning in a waterfowl guide's kitchen.

Many of my fondest outdoor memories have more to do with food than with fish caught or game killed. Though it's been years, I still remember the "Great Fairfield Oyster

Orgy" that followed a day of goose hunting at Mattamuskeet when my dad made the ill-advised offer to buy me all
the oysters I could eat. I had 'em raw, steamed, stewed, and
fried and even managed to stuff a couple of oyster fritters
just barely past my vocal cords before staggering outside. I
was so full I was afraid to bend over to get in the car.

Then there was the time I made chili on a trout-fishing
expedition. While my two fishing buddies watched with interest, I tossed a double handful of chili powder and red
pepper into the iron pot with the beef, tomatoes, onions,
and beans. We left it simmering over a low fire while we scattered out to fish the stream. The whole valley reeked of chili,
and when we returned, I raised the lid for a quick sniff and
promptly lost most of the hair in my nose. One of my companions credited that chili with curing a congenital sinus
condition.

There was also that cold October day with a stinging rain
riding a stiff northeast wind when I stood alone on the end
of an ocean pier plugging for bluefish. After a while, two
fishermen joined me, and I could see right away that they
were better prepared than I was for this kind of fishing by
a long shot—not to mention numerous short ones. After
taking a couple of nips from a suspicious jar, they set about
lighting a small charcoal grill they'd brought.

While one tended the grill, the other began fishing. He
launched a wobbly cast into the teeth of the gale, and every
time his lure hit the water, a two-pound bluefish grabbed it.
The cook split each fish, slung out the innards, and placed
it skin up on the grill. My new friends graciously offered me
grill space for my blues and a snort for my health. During
the next hour, we caught and ate perhaps a dozen crisp, delicious blues, and my health was so improved that when I
finally judged it prudent to leave, I merely leaned back on
the wind and sailed down the pier to a safe port.

An appreciation for oysters, chili, and grilled bluefish is
not hard to understand. What is less easy to explain is the
sportsman's fascination with the kind of food one finds in a
country store. A person of impeccable breeding, exquisite

manners, and unquestionable taste will gorge on the most incredible array of swill after following a brace of bird dogs all morning.

If you have never dined in a four-star country store, you are culturally deprived. There is, of course, no *Michelin Guide* to assist you in the selection of a good one, but I can tell you what I look for. It has been my experience that the food is better in those country stores where the driveway is paved with old bottle caps, relieved by a single, rusty gas pump. In the dusty front window, you should find at least one very old movie card advertising a double feature starring the likes of Tom Mix, Lash LaRue, or the Durango Kid.

Once inside, it is proper to nod to the maître d', who likely will be propped against the counter in his overalls, working a toothpick into some remote cavity. Other diners may already be seated on upended drink crates around a potbellied stove, pouring peanuts into their soft drinks and spitting tobacco juice on the stove to hear it sizzle.

In order to savor the experience, one must not hurry. Pause and breath deeply, sorting out the various scents of fertilizer, seed, leather, dust, and tired feet. Look around. On the wall, you will find everything from harnesses to hankies, Barlow knives to radiator belts. You may even find something you've always wanted, like a little perfumed chenille skunk to hang from your rearview mirror to mask the musk of working mutts. My favorite store has a sign on the wall that reads: "We will crank your car and hold your baby, but we sell for cash and don't mean maybe."

Sniff the jars of pickled eggs, sausages, and pig's feet, and sample each. You will not be immediately sorry. I cannot, literally, recommend too highly any tins of hash you might find—I found two buckshot in a can once. If you're lucky, there may even be a keg of salt herring. On the counter will almost surely be a wheel of greasy rat cheese. Buy a slab. Even if you don't like cheese, it may help offset any unpleasantries occasioned by your other choices.

On the shelves will be cans of Vienna sausages, salmon, tuna, sardines, and potted meat. (If you're ever fortunate enough to visit Vienna, however, be aware that the natives don't call it "Vy-eenie.") Avoid reading the label on the potted meat unless you are uncommonly interested in the final disposition of pork snouts, beef hearts, stomachs, lips, ears, and a variety of less distinguished cuts. Elsewhere, you will find nabs, wrapped sandwiches of questionable age, twelve-gauge peppermint sticks, candy bars, cookies in jars, and a vast assortment of cupcakes, raisin cookies, cinnamon buns, and pies.

I have one hunting companion whose favorite country store lunch is a large can of whole, peeled tomatoes and a watery chocolate drink. My own taste runs heavily to dill pickles, rat cheese, potted meat scooped out of the can with peanut butter nabs, cold pork 'n beans, orange soft drinks, and coconut candy bars.

Once, while several of us were dining at a country store, my son Scott noted that his can of pork 'n beans contained only a single, small chunk of fatty pork. "That is to be expected," explained Joe Phillips. "There is never more than one chunk of pork in a can; otherwise, they would have to call it 'porks 'n beans.'"

As I have said, I'm not sure I truly understand the almost universal appeal to sportsmen of meals of this nature, but if I had to guess, I would say that it reflects some primeval lust for independence. As a kid, I was constantly being reprimanded for squandering my allowance on similar items in the neighborhood grocery instead of forthrightly facing the daily onslaught of boiled cabbages, collards, rutabagas, and snap beans thought necessary for proper growth.

Perhaps it is the shuddering recollection of a pot of snaps simmered all day in grease that drives me across the bottle caps and over the threshold to the herring keg and potted meat. I only know that once there, I am in the midst of gastronomic glory. And sometimes, as I sit contentedly watching a cutthroat game of checkers, I feel moved to offer a critique.

"That was," I might say, "a good pig's foot, but not a great pig's foot."

A
POCKETFUL
OF
PLEASURE

It's a sobering experience to discover that you are among the few surviving practitioners of a custom once common throughout the land. When, for example, did people stop carrying pocketknives? I have carried some sort of small folding knife since I was seven or eight years old—some fifty years—and until recently, I never encountered anyone who thought it strange. Now, all of a sudden, I'm beginning to feel like the penultimate, if not the last, Mohican.

Historically, the adult male who didn't have a blade quite literally couldn't cut it, socially or otherwise. The Barlow knife is practically symbolic of the nation's work ethic, and even the most prominent businessmen once carried a small penknife on the odd chance that a fingernail might need paring. Long before we had anything else to put in them, pockets carried knives. The 5,000-year-old fur-clad man whose body was recently found frozen in a glacier had a knife. No mention was made of any car keys or loose change.

My grandfather always carried a pocketknife, and I still have it along with at least a dozen more I've accumulated over the years. Like old friends, they are happy to make themselves useful. I like the way they look and feel, and I like to sharpen them on winter evenings. It is sweet, mindless labor.

Admittedly, I've had suspicions that the practice of carrying a knife might be eroding. People in the office invariably borrow my knife whenever there's a package to be opened or a string to be cut. And kids are often astonished to discover that a seemingly mild-mannered pre-geezer is packing a shiv. Even some campers have abandoned knives for expensive multipurpose tools that offer thirty-five options from a toothpick to a socket wrench—and maybe a blade if they could only find it.

When I made a cross-country flight a few years ago, I arrived at the metal detector and dutifully emptied my pockets into a tray. One item was a small three-blade stockman, a common style of pocketknife. It caught the eye of a young guard.

"Is that a buck knife?" he asked.

"Well, the Buck company made it," I replied, a bit confused.

"This airline doesn't permit you to carry a buck knife onboard," I was told. "You'll have to leave it behind."

It turned out that this particular airline prohibited the carrying aboard of what it described as any buck-style knife. It soon became clear that the airline's intent was to ban large folding knives of the type used to skin deer (and possibly pilots and flight attendants). Because the Buck Knife Company had pioneered fine folding, lockback knives of this type years ago, its brand had become a generic tag for all such knives. This left me in the awkward position of trying to explain that not every Buck knife is a buck knife, and I was making no headway until an older guard came over. He glanced at my little knife and waved me through with a weary smile.

I was fortunate to have encountered a fellow who had peeled an apple, spread potted meat on a square nab, cleaned a squirrel, sharpened a pencil, sliced a fig, dug out a splinter, cut fishing line, or taken care of one of the countless other daily chores only a pocketknife can handle. But even he seemed resigned to a losing cause.

On the hopeful notion that pocketknives will continue to be appreciated for their many practical and nonthreatening services, let me share a few prejudices. I prefer three-bladed knives, and I use the longer clip blade to clean fish, cut bait, smear mayonnaise, whatever. The stubby spey blade gets the rougher tasks more likely to dull the edge, while I reserve the third small blade for emergencies and keep it extremely sharp.

These days, the blades of most commercial-grade pocket-knives are made of stainless steel, and the old problems of extreme hardness and brittleness have been largely over-come. Many modern stainless steels will hold a good edge and they don't rust. The best steel I've seen in store-bought, American-made pocketknives is 440C, although some cus-tom—mostly fixed-blade—knives feature superior steels, in-cluding variations of Damascus, at fancy prices. I still like carbon steel blades, but very few quality pocketknives with such blades are made in the United States anymore. For-tunately, some superb German pocketknives are available with good Solingen steel blades. Carbon steel will rust, of course, but if it is wiped off after use and oiled occasionally, it will develop a handsome patina.

Check to make sure the blades don't wobble even slightly when open (that's one reason I don't recommend buying mail-order knives). Look for solid brass or nickel silver bol-sters, sturdy handles, and other obvious signs of quality. Stag handles are handsome, traditional, and durable, but expect to pay a premium for them.

To sharpen blades, a soft Arkansas stone will remove steel quickly; however, synthetic stones like Crystolon or fine India are excellent and they're more durable than soft Ar-kansas. If you want to give the edge a final polish, a hard Arkansas stone is hard to beat (expensive, but worth it). Avoid Carborundum and any stone shorter than about six inches. A good sharpening method is to advance the blade across the stone as though you were cutting a shallow slice, maintaining the same angle with each stroke. Start with a dozen careful strokes on one side before turning the blade over for an equal number of return strokes, then repeat the process. Use plenty of honing oil. As the proper bevel be-gins to form on each side, make fewer strokes on each side until you can no longer feel a burr along the edge. I find that a hand-held magnifying glass—the type used to view photographic slides—is helpful.

Now put the knife in your pocket. This is one tradition we need to keep.

MEAN
STREETS
AND TOUGH
CRITTERS

The sparrow was sitting in the middle of a downtown street, taking advantage of a momentary lull in traffic. As I approached in my car, I expected to see the bird flit away at the last moment. That's the game these tough city birds seem to like to play.

But this sparrow never moved, and by the time I realized it was not going to fly, it was too late to stop or dodge. Must be sick or injured, I thought as I came to a near stop and looked back. The sparrow was still in the road, pecking away intently at something. I watched it for a few moments until it finished eating and flew away. That bird plainly didn't care that I had straddled it in a moving automobile.

How did that sparrow resist the urge to fly as the car passed overhead? Was this a learned response, or had this bird simply been born unafraid into a world where automobiles are as much a part of its natural habitat as a tree or a fireplug? Had I seen a mutant "early bird" that would pass its survival adaptation to future offspring in one of those infrequent evolutionary lurches, or had I merely seen a bold sparrow with "Adapt or Die" tattooed on its shoulder?

The author of *Wildlife in North Carolina*'s popular ongoing "Nature's Ways" column didn't seem surprised when I told him what I'd seen. "The way things are going," Larry Earley mused, "in another 1,000 years, street sparrows may be driving cars and we may be pecking in the road."

For many years, I have lived in an inner-city neighborhood only a few minutes from Raleigh's downtown. An amazing wildlife population lives around me amid lawn mowers, traffic, loud music, gangs of kids, dogs, and house-cats that hunt tirelessly.

Just next door, a raccoon waltzed through the cat door one day and muscled in to feed from the dish alongside the felines. Until steps were taken to keep it out, it quickly learned where the food bag was kept and no doubt would have been opening the refrigerator and making its own peanut butter and jelly sandwiches within a week. Another neighbor who tired of what she thought was a marauding raccoon that kept raiding her garbage cans borrowed traps from the city and wound up catching an entire family, including kids, nieces, aunts, and grandparents.

After coons learned to open the wire handles on the lid of my garbage can, I bought a more secure system. Now the unyielding lid has been so thoroughly chewed around the edges that it looks like a lace doily. These raccoons even leave me bones and scraps from other garbage cans. I think their intention is to guide me in my eating habits so that I will leave more desirable garbage.

Just this past week, a possum I encountered in my drive-way asked me what the heck I thought I was doing coming home so late. Cottontails are having lawn parties up and down the street. Chipmunks have carved out interstate highways under the ivy, and moles have excavated a sub-way system throughout the backyard. Southern flying squirrels are practicing trapeze acts in the treetops, and there are so many gray squirrels hereabouts that they're having gang wars with blue jays, cardinals, and myriad songbirds at the bird feeders. Even tiny, elusive mammals like shrews can occasionally be seen as they go about their customary business of eating many times their body weight in daily prey.

Other species I see occasionally include hawks, bats, skinks, toads, and garter snakes. On summer nights when I leave the windows open, I often wake to a muted chorus of great horned and screech owls. And though they aren't in my immediate neighborhood, white-tailed deer, muskrats, and beavers live within the city limits.

There is a simple explanation for this apparent wildlife explosion in our cities. These animals have been able to adapt to the habitats they find in urban areas. Indeed, their landscape of concrete, roads, shopping centers, and housing developments is the only habitat on earth that is actually increasing. Wetlands, tallgrass prairies, old-growth forests, rain forests, tundra, potholes, estuaries, and myriad other priceless habitats are dwindling steadily—some may literally disappear within our lifetimes. Gone with them will be the countless plants and animals that lived there. Those animals can't simply move elsewhere because most wildlife habitat already supports its maximum occupancy. Gone, too, will be the benefits to weather, medicine, and other life forces that these habitats provide, and we will someday wish we'd handled them more wisely.

Most of us love our neighborhood wildlife, of course, but their prosperity is not a sign that all is well. We may be living among the few animals that have a long-term future.

OUT ON
MANEUVERS

Every military tactician has a pet theory to explain the effi-
cient resolution of that Desert Storm business a few years
back—superior airpower, Patriot missiles, better-trained
troops. But could it be that this late unpleasantness reached
a hasty conclusion partly because there are no fish to catch
in the desert?

It's a little-known fact—and may even be top secret—that
military personnel rank second only to firefighters as avid
fishermen. Despite a notoriously rigorous schedule, military folks get time off just like the rest of us. And they get
to take it in some far-flung places with interesting angling
opportunities.

When I was serving Uncle Sam, I quickly learned that one
of the first things you do when you get a new assignment is
consult maps and MAAG (Military Anglers Advisory Group)
to learn the off-duty potential at your new station.

When I reported to Fort Holabird in Baltimore in the
mid-1960s, my new boss—a full, bird colonel—called me to
his office, where I sat nervously while he reviewed my personnel file. After several tense minutes, he reached the sec-
tion that listed my hobbies. Tossing the file aside, he grinned
and asked me when I thought I could get a free weekend to
go largemouth bass fishing with him on Maryland's Eastern
Shore.

That was not my first inkling that life in the army might
not be all spit and polish. A year earlier, during summer
training, I had drawn KP a couple of days while our company was on field maneuvers in Virginia. After the potatoes
were peeled, we had some free time. Most of my exhausted
fellow pot washers took naps, but I fished a stream that hap-

pened to run past the obstacle course. Less than a hundred yards away, muddy recruits were crawling under barbed wire and live machine-gun fire while I caught smallmouth bass. I decided I was pressing my luck when an unarmed rocket landed in the middle of the creek.

The colonel loved that story. It reminded him of a trout stream in Germany he'd fished in 1945 while Allied troops were still tidying up pockets of resistance. His problem wasn't matching the hatch; it was dodging sniper fire.

At Fort Holabird, I met John Iwanowski, who worked at the post as a civilian, and he encouraged me to join the Baltimore Anglers Club. It was a small group, but its twenty-some members must surely rank among the most obsessed anglers in history. They included Lefty Kreh, a night watchman at Fort Detrick who has since become the reigning international guru of fly fishing, and Boyd Pfeiffer, an anatomy student who later became outdoor editor of the *Washington Post* and authored countless articles and several fishing books. Likewise, Charley McTee and Joe Reynolds have both become successful outdoor writers. Another, Jack Goellner, became director of the Johns Hopkins University Press. Our mentor was the late Joe Brooks, an honorary member and Baltimore native who was then angling editor of *Outdoor Life*.

Falling in with such a bunch was a dream come true. In early spring, we'd fish the shad runs in the Susquehanna River and Rappahannock. Above Conowingo Dam, we caught largemouth and smallmouth bass. The Upper Potomac sometimes yielded fifty or more smallmouth a day on flies, and even then, Lefty could throw an entire ninety-foot flyline *without* the rod! On Chesapeake Bay, we crabbed and fished for stripers and yellow perch. Mayfly time took us to Big Hunting Creek in western Maryland for trout or to the Letort and Yellow Breeches limestone streams at Carlisle, Pennsylvania.

Of course, I realize that I was fortunate to have served during a time of peace—Vietnam was just heating up. It would have been far different under other circumstances. I was also lucky to have served in an administrative outfit whose unofficial motto was "Retreat Hell, Backspace!" But during those two years, I came to appreciate the appeal of a military career that blended hard work, pride in public service, good friends, and superb fishing.

Even after I completed active duty, the armed forces offered occasional opportunities to wet a line in out-of-the-way places. At summer camp one year, my unit flew to Camp McCoy, Wisconsin, where we spent two unseasonably torrid weeks in classes. After five o'clock, however, we were free to pursue our pleasure. Most found little to do, but I quickly located a sandy-bottomed stream that ran through the camp. It was full of wild brown trout. At the end of training, 269 reservists had the opportunity to vote on whether to return to Camp McCoy for the following year's training or go back to Fort Knox. The vote was 268 to 1 in favor of Knox. I think the colonel would have made it 267 to 2.

Is it any wonder that I suspect the lack of a good trout stream in those Persian Gulf States might have been added incentive to get the job done quickly?

BULLETS
FACE
FORWARD

The very notion that I might attempt to help someone become a better rifle and pistol shot will be a source of entertainment in some circles. Friends who have witnessed my skill with a shotgun will be especially amused. Yet I need not point out that we are buffeted on all fronts these days by "experts" who speak authoritatively, and at length, on all manner of subjects that they have not personally mastered or even attempted. It is the signature of the 1990s.

That said, I must confess that I am, indeed, a poor shot with a scattergun. Furthermore, I no longer shoot very often or particularly well with a rifle or pistol. Ah, but there was a time. At the Virginia Military Institute in the early 1960s, and later at Forts Knox, Benjamin Harrison, and Holabird, the army took a keen interest in teaching young officers the rudiments of rifle and pistol shooting. Those of us who had spent our early years wearing out air rifles on tin cans and hunting squirrels with .22 single-shots were quick learners, while those with urban backgrounds had to overcome an irrational fear of firearms and start from scratch.

I recall a grizzled old sergeant who was patiently showing a group how to load the magazine of a .45-caliber semiautomatic service pistol. One raw second lieutenant was having trouble getting the bullets into the magazine, so the sergeant paused to help him. Returning to his podium, the sergeant sarcastically amended his instructions with the air of one who had just witnessed a new level of incompetence. "Bullets face forward, gentlemen," he said dryly.

That sergeant, and countless other unflappable range officers, taught us how to shoot a variety of weapons, particularly the M-1 Garand rifle and the standard-issue .45 side-arm. Most of us eventually became acceptably proficient, and some excelled. Many of us never forgot those basic skills and later, as civilians, found them valuable in hunting game or target shooting.

Even if you've had the advantage of military instruction, you would surely find it helpful to take a refresher course to reacquaint yourself with sound shooting techniques. I suspect, for example, that modern big-game hunters would be particularly well served to learn how to use stable positions and a rifle sling to steady their shots. That's too big a subject to address here, but two other bits of information could greatly improve your shooting this season. The first tactic will help you gain a steady sight picture and a smooth release with rifle or pistol, with or without a scope.

Many shooters don't know how to settle down and make a telling shot—they rush the process while their adrenaline is pumping, jerk the trigger, flinch, and wonder why they scatter bullets all over the target and beyond.

My old military instructors had the answer. They told us to remember the acronym BRASS, which stood for Breathe, Relax, Aim, Squeeze, Shoot. Once we were in our stance and ready to shoot, they advised us to carefully think about, and follow, the same sequence with every shot. First, take a moderate breath and let out half of it. Second, make a determined effort to relax, and only then begin to concentrate on lining up the sights. When you're satisfied you're on target, begin to slowly squeeze the trigger.

"If you're doing this correctly, you will not know precisely when the gun will fire," we were told. "The last step—Shoot—is the only step in the sequence that is not predetermined. If you don't consciously try to make the gun shoot, you are less likely to jerk or flinch."

It works. Try it on the target range until the sequence becomes second nature. Naturally, it works best on stationary targets, but once you've made the process a rapid habit, it will aid all your shots, even at moving game.

I've found another military tip particularly helpful, especially with open sights. When you're lining up rear and front sights, you tend to focus your vision on the target. Big mistake. The key is to focus on the sights—particularly the rear sight—making sure both are aligned properly, while blurring the target beyond. If your sight picture is lined up correctly, your chances of making a good shot are excellent, even if you're having trouble holding rock steady. Proper focus and alignment will occur instantaneously and habitually with practice, and it does not mean that you can't see or identify your target.

Now, go forth and shoot safely and well. And remember: bullets face forward.

THE
BIRD
AT
HAND

No one I know comes right out and says so, but lots of hunters seem to think of the mourning dove as some sort of second-rate harbinger, a Tom and Jerry cartoon or Movietone News bird that provides momentary entertainment until the main feature gets cranked up. Hickory shad share this unfortunate status with doves, ascending swollen rivers in early spring, where they serve as a brief preamble to another fishing season. A handful of other harbingers get even less respect. Blue-winged teal often pass through so early that they are barely noticed, and the premature surf fisherman's season advances behind a vast infantry of skates and toadfish.

It is not, alas, the arrival of green-eyed puffers, bluewings, shad, and September migrants that most of us celebrate; it's what they foreshadow. If they are finally here, can bobwhites, trout, grouse, bass, ducks, salmon, deer, bluefish, African buffalo—serious stuff—be far behind? Whether it's fair or not, sportsmen tend to regard all forerunners as warm-ups, light-hitting leadoff batters, mere foreplay.

I used to feel this way about the opening of dove season, but less so nowadays. One of the happier things that accompanies the patina of fifty-plus years is the realization that foreplay, in all its various manifestations, is the real game. Once you make the alarming discovery that the ultimate goal of life is death, you stop licking your lips over what's next and begin to settle down in the present. The simple truth is that *Zenaidura macroura carolinensis* in season, and in range, is more than enough immediate challenge for anyone.

I didn't always understand this. When I first began to hunt doves at the age of ten with my father and grandfather, the appeal was raw and basic. Dove season afforded the unparalleled opportunity to shoot at a lot of targets, and Dad was buying the shells. It was fast fun and good practice. I had no sense that planning, clever tactics, and good dogs might enhance the sport. Later on, my dove shooting evolved into the quasi-social event that has been traditional throughout much of this migratory bird's range, especially the Southeast.

Every August just before the opening of dove season, a gentleman farmer with lots of big fields will harvest his early corn, being just sloppy enough with the machinery to stay on the legal side of the baiting laws. Then he will invite all his kinfolk and friends—and their friends too—the theory being that big fields require ample hunters to keep birds moving. I have gotten engraved invitations to these things.

Corn on the cob simmers in a huge kettle, and buckets of coleslaw are placed on long tables under the trees. Hush puppies, biscuits, or rolls are piled high, and a deep dish of banana pudding is set out, where it soon achieves the consistency of caulking compound. Sweet tea is dipped from gallon jugs and poured over ice from coolers. A gutted but otherwise whole 90- to 140-pound young pig is cooked most of the day over hickory, and when it's ready, we gather around to gnaw the ribs and pick at the tenderloins and hams until there's nothing left but a pile of bones and a great, greasy flap of skin. Most often the meal is served at midday, but leftovers are revisited and iced tea is no longer the only libation at dusk after the shotguns are unloaded. Of course, the "unloaded" rule is not enforced on those non-hunting guests whose definition of a shooter has nothing to do with guns.

At legal shooting time, hunters begin to take up stands around the fields. Some are camouflaged and seek modest cover under trees, in hedgerows, or along weedy edges, while others in white shirts and blaze-orange caps choose to sit on folding stools in short stubble at high mid-field. Their belief—often proved accurate on opening day at least—is that if the doves are using that field, they will come even if you are dressed like Clarabelle the clown and sitting atop an elephant decorated for a holy day in Burma—which, considering the customary 90-degree heat and 98 percent humidity in early September, would not seem totally out of place.

This is not nearly as dangerous as it sounds. Shooters ritually decline low shots and aren't spooked by the occasional spatter of spent shot falling on nearby leaves. On opening day and for a few days beyond, shooting the limit is common, even for those whose skills go unhoned from one opening day to the next.

Manufacturers of shotgun shells love this bird. It is not unusual to run through three boxes of shells in an afternoon and still be four birds shy of the limit. Odd, too, that the lean Mach II missile that whistles in at twelve o'clock noon over cut corn and pines is the same corpulent creature that only days before was vacuuming seeds at your bird feeder. What miracle transforms pullet to bullet? Given that your chances are about the same as trying to spray a low-flying F-18 with a garden hose, it's a wonder that anyone has ever tasted a succulent dove breast wrapped in bacon and grilled over hot coals.

This kind of dove hunting is great fun, and no season would be complete without at least one extravagant shoot. Yet with opportunities becoming more limited even in the South, the traditional social shoot survives more and more on large, pay-to-hunt farms where choice cornfields are either harvested to attract early-season doves or planted in sunflowers especially for that purpose. The shooting can be as torrid as the weather and a hearty meal is still often served, but such events cater largely to urban sportsmen more likely to shoot the first week and forget all about doves the rest of the year. Indeed, the big shoots only superficially resemble the kind of full-season dove hunting that I have come to anticipate.

It is the end of August, a day before the opener, and Mike Gaddis and I are on the back roads of eastern North Carolina in his twenty-year-old, rocker-rusted Chevy truck. It is godawful hot. Under the shell in the back is Squaw's dog box filled with fresh hay—but no dog this trip. Today we carry binoculars, a set of county road maps, a water jug, and a mental list of farms, friends, and acquaintances. If we find promising fields and know the landowners, a call that evening will gain us entry. If not, we stop at the nearest farmhouse and ask. We're wearing our usual jeans—country come to country—no fancy Safari shirts or club patches. Style is not our style, nor would it be smart for this purpose. Back before Mike retired to his farm, he even removed the city tags from his truck before we made these preseason scouting trips. Because we're polite, promise to leave no shell piles or trash, close gates, and avoid shooting toward houses or barns, we usually get permission to hunt. But mostly, I suspect, it's because we do not act, think, or look like outsiders.

Mike pulls off on the shoulder and we scan the backs of fields, especially where corn has just been harvested. Early in the afternoon, we don't expect to see many birds flying, so we're looking for doves in trees, especially dead snags, or the occasional pair trading through a gap or fluttering down to feed. A powerline pegged with a dozen noonday dozers is always promising. Once, years earlier, we glassed a field that was so full of feeding doves that their moving mass looked as though someone were shaking out a huge gray flannel quilt.

Harvested corn is the prime attractant for mourning doves throughout most of their range, but it's not the only one. Mike and I have found birds in vast numbers feeding on what, to the unpracticed eye, would seem to be highly unlikely fare—cucumbers and melons, wheat, sunflowers, even cotton. Mourning doves dearly love the seeds splitting out of rotting cukes, cantaloupes, and watermelons. Sunflowers are legendary for their appeal and are planted now more than ever. The right cotton field, neglected and weedy between the rows and along the edges, may be lousy with small seeds from croton. Croton is commonly called dove weed for good reason.

On one occasion, we had a tip that the Feds had plowed under a twenty-acre field of ripe marijuana. The doves kept coming that day; was it my imagination that they seemed to drift in with an uncharacteristic I-don't-give-a-damn attitude? We set up our stands along a hedgerow, laid out some tie-dyed T-shirts and a box of incense, and cranked up the Grateful Dead. Business was very good.

Early-season scouting is rewarding, but scouting also pays off throughout the season, the big advantage being that you can immediately hunt concentrations of birds you find. Unlike the large social shoots, this hunting is best done solo or with one or two serious companions who have learned that the game changes dramatically after opening day. By mid-September doves become increasingly wary and scattered, and as the weather continues to cool, they lose their loyalty to even the choicest fields, often leaving for good after the first flurry of shooting. We put on camouflage and choose stands under observed flight lines, making sure there's cover to hide us. We build quick, rough blinds when necessary, and sometimes hang confidence dove decoys on nearby bare limbs.

Today, of course, we're still one day shy of legal shooting, but we find what we're looking for—doves trading in and out of a small cornfield tucked between a pine woods and a pond on a farm we already have permission to hunt. The layout is ideal—it has proven itself in the past—and we know that the brushy cover around the pond is going to be the best spot to set up. We're back at noon the following day and have it all to ourselves. Shooting is slow at first, but by mid-afternoon, the birds begin to come. Characteristically, there is a brief flurry, followed by a thirty-minute lull. By 4:30, there are fewer and shorter lulls, gun barrels are hot, and Squaw is busy. Mostly she is retrieving Mike's birds because I am averaging my usual one bird out of three or four shots.

At sundown, we clean our birds while sitting on the tailgate. The town of Newton Grove lies a dozen miles up the road, but I am nearly certain I can smell oysters frying at Henry's. I mention this to Mike. "Probably smell a lemon meringue pie too," he says.

Such hunts make me wonder about sportsmen who consider the mourning dove a mere songbird, unworthy of notice were it not the first target of the season. As we drive to Henry's, I remember a bright, crisp afternoon late in the second portion of one dove season when Mike and I drove out a two-lane blacktop south of Raleigh to check a spot we knew about. As we topped the hill, we could see the powerline over the field sagging with doves.

We took stands on the crest of a small rise, our silhouettes broken by hastily stacked cornstalks. Mike and Squaw sat back-to-back about twenty yards away, close enough for me to see her shiver every time a dove approached from her direction—a signal she and Mike had long ago perfected. The doves sailed in rosy-breasted in the late autumn sunlight, and we had our limits in an hour. We unloaded our guns and sat silently amid the lightly rattling stalks watching the clouds turn pink, then crimson, then dark gray.

Squaw had seen many of those incoming birds before either of us spotted them, and as usual, she had found every bird we shot. Certainly it would never have occurred to her to look beyond doves to the duck season that would follow. She lived to hunt the bird in season, and Mike and I have learned to do the same.

THE
NEUSE
UNDER
FALLS

Back before the Falls Lake dam was built, which flooded the upper Neuse to provide water for the growing state capital, this stretch of river was nearly wild. You could drift for miles without seeing any sign of habitation. One brilliant November blue-sky day in 1974 after we had learned of plans to dam the river, Mike Gaddis and I loaded our gear into a twelve-foot johnboat below the NC 50 bridge north of Raleigh and pushed off to pay our last respects.

The river stretched before us, a winding, dark artery broken by occasional chuckling riffles. Lofty sycamores leaned out over the remarkably clear pools, forming a corridor of stark white columns that were reflected in the water amid lingering smears of yellow, red, and rust from the hardwoods. Even though the fall colors were mostly gone, it was a sight as handsome as any I had ever seen.

Mike's plan was to drift and hunt squirrels as he had often done here in the past, but I had been unable to resist the notion that bass and panfish would surely be active in such Indian summer weather, so I had arrived with both a shotgun and a spinning rod.

"You're just going to scare off the squirrels flailing the water with that thing," Mike said, but it was a futile, good-natured objection. We had long ago recognized that our sporting preferences aren't entirely identical, and while we tease each other from time to time, we have come to the tolerant understanding that all hunting and fishing is good when it is done in magical places.

Two hundred yards downstream—just opposite the spot

where public boat ramps and a huge parking lot would soon be built on the new lake—we came to a sharp bend where the wooded bank on our right rose steeply.

"Look there," pointed Mike. "That hillside is covered with native laurel. Not many people realize how prevalent it is this far from the mountains, yet it is common along many Piedmont rivers. Wish you had seen it in bloom."

The first gray squirrel we had seen was sitting on a stump at eye level just beyond the bend, seemingly unconcerned by our passage.

"It has always amazed me that squirrels are seldom spooked by a boat," whispered Mike. "Sometimes, if you're quiet, you can drift within a few yards, but if you attempt to get out on the bank, they skedaddle." Since that target provided no challenge, Mike moved to the bank, eased out of the boat, and took his shot as the squirrel raced through the treetops.

Between bushytails, I paddled and made casts across the dark pools with a small spinner. Robin and small bass struck on nearly every cast, and even Mike was impressed. Swapping paddling chores occasionally, we continued to drift southeast toward our takeout spot at the NC 98 bridge, where we had left Mike's truck.

About halfway through our passage, we came to an even more handsome stretch of river where sandy bars and huge rocks diverted the river from its meandering course. Tall rock cliffs soared over us on the left, and we pulled the boat up on a sandbar to have a look. "This is called Zeagle's Rock," said Mike. "There are caves here, and I have often thought that Native Americans must have had a special affection for this spot for thousands of years. Good shelter, good swimming, good hunting . . ."

"And good fishing," I said.

"That too," Mike allowed.

Late in the afternoon, with the shadows growing longer and several squirrels in Mike's game bag, we put aside our guns and fishing gear and slowly paddled the final mile or so in silence. When the bridge came in sight, Mike turned the canoe so that we could take a final look upstream while we

drifted the last few hundred yards. I knew what he was thinking—I won't ever do this again, won't ever see this again.
Nor, very soon, will anyone else, and most people will never
know what has been lost.

In recent years, Mike and I have spent a fair amount
of time fishing Falls Lake from Mike's bass boat. It's a big,
comfortable boat with a 175-horsepower Mercury, trolling
motor, pedestal seats fore and aft, and even a fancy marine
AM-FM so we can listen to music while we fish.

Sometimes we drift past the exposed top of Zeagle's
Rock, working soft plastic salamanders or pig 'n jigs down
the steep sides into . . . what? Are there big bass or only
watery ghosts in those caves now?

A couple of years ago, not far from this spot, Mike caught
a largemouth that weighed over eleven pounds. He was very
happy about that, but I wonder if he wouldn't swap both
boat and bass for the river we saw that day twenty-five years
ago.

WHEN
HONEYBUNS
GO BAD

"Save the best for last" is an old, old saying that probably goes back to our Puritan roots and may even have a more ancient origin—a Roman orgy comes to mind. Yielding to the fatuous natterings of flocks of forebears, most of us have obediently saved the best for last for so many years that it would never occur to us to question the wisdom of delayed indulgence. Some of us have saved the "best" so long that it's gone bad.

We wear old clothes while new ones gather mildew in the closet. We instinctively eat the broken cookies first and save the biggest with the most chocolate chips for last. We write thank you notes on school notepaper and save the good stationery—for what? If we're fortunate enough to have china, crystal, or nice linens, do we use them regularly? Of course not. We eat off the chipped plates we bought with coupons at the grocery store and drink out of plastic Durham Bulls' cups or chug from the jug straight out of the refrigerator.

Of course, it is virtuous and satisfying to live a simple, frugal life. Someday, we will get a gold star (at least) if we keep squeezing all those little soap remnants together to make one squishy bar. Yet carried to extremes, this is an insidious habit, and those of us who hunt and fish are no less guilty. It is no coincidence that exceptionally fine bamboo fly rods or high-quality guns—especially collectible shotguns—are called "closet queens." As for me, I'm still wearing my grandfather's hunting clothes. I broke in my boots at Fort Knox forty years ago, and I've still got the spare pair hanging in the basement, spit-shined and ready for inspection. I own boxes containing hundreds of virgin trout flies and bass bugs, yet I invariably choose to fish with a veteran, paint-chipped popper or a fly so thoroughly chewed and matted that it's virtually unrecognizable.

You can therefore imagine my consternation when I recently read some advice offered by a man who had survived a shipwreck and drifted alone in a raft for weeks before being rescued. "I knew I might not have long to live, and I durn sure wasn't going to shortchange myself," he said. "I had a small supply of food and water, and I rationed it to make it last. But each time I ate or drank anything, I picked not only the freshest food from the stock that was left, but also the stuff I liked most. That way, no matter how rotten or rancid the supplies got, I was always eating the best of them. There wasn't much I could do while I was waiting to be rescued, but that little act of rebellion gave me some pleasure. Besides, if I had saved the best for last, I would have resigned myself to consuming the worst food right from the beginning, and even the stuff that started out fresh would have been spoiled by the time I got around to it. It made no sense whatever."

Here is a man who has discovered a simple, myth-busting truth, and it's about time too. We are all awash in that derelict raft we call life, and there are no guarantees that we will be afloat tomorrow. It's enough to make those of us on the cusp of geezerhood change our ways. After all, our kids already live by the modern rationale that "life is short; eat dessert first."

I can't abandon all my bad habits, but I have been making a few modest changes. I've begun wearing my good suit pants for no particular reason (and I'm training myself to accept this as the best reason). I'm drinking the good wine first—maybe I'll get lucky and someone else who outlives me can deal with the rotgut. I'm going for the most flawless apple in the basket, the crispest French fry on the plate, and the most heavily glazed honeybun in the rack. The good guns are going afield this year, and vacation is over for those perfect popping bugs. What, after all, have I been saving them for?

It's not as easy as it sounds, and I'm sure to slip up occasionally. This fall, I caught myself tying on a previously used Wulff Royal even though it was one of those bright fall days when the leaves are ablaze and the trout are on the move. Furthermore, I knew it might be my last trip of the season, or ever. "What are you doing?" I said to myself. "Here you are on the most glorious day of the year, and you're about to fish with the worst fly you own." I clipped off the old fly and replaced it with the most pristine and perfectly proportioned Wulff in the box.

But try as I might, I couldn't bring myself to throw the old one away. Instead, I put it in a corner of my fly box. It's possible that I might live long enough to get down to my last fly. If so, I've got one.

OCCONEECHEE'S
RIVER
TREASURE

If I travel the thread of memory back to the early 1950s, I come to the dark isolation of Occoneechee Neck, rumors of buried Confederate silver, and the sleepy warmth of a backseat as we skirt the dark woods and swamps on US 158 in Northampton County. It is a late afternoon in winter, and my nose is pressed against the cold glass as we pass through Jackson, where strings of colored lights sag across the road.

Just west of town, we pass a tall abandoned house, its black windows overlooking huge cotton fields that stretch to the far woods. A few tiny blue lights mark a distant tenant house. At the head of the long curve just before we reach the millpond with its black water and shaggy cypress, we pass a road that slants to the left.

"Goes down into the Neck," says Dad.

I know about the Neck, or I think I do. It is a brooding place of murk and monster, populated by the ghosts of Confederate officers and a young black boy who stumbles onto a long-lost treasure. It is more than enough to tantalize me, though I have seen only this watery finger at Boone's Mill, where we cross Gumberry Swamp. Much of what I believe about the Neck, as I learn much later, is imagination—mine and, more especially, Mebane Holoman Burgwyn's.

A few miles south of Weldon, the Roanoke River makes a sweeping curve that describes and isolates Occoneechee Neck, a place with a unique blend of history, diverse wildlife, priceless wetlands, unusual riverine typography, and people, some of whom have owned and farmed land here for 200 years. That much is fact, but it does not bury my ghost.

So, on a cool, overcast day this past November, Merrill Lynch and my son, Scott, and I turn south off US 158 onto SR 1128—one of two roads into the Neck—and begin to explore. Merrill is an avid birder who works for the Nature Conservancy. Like me, he grew up in nearby Roanoke Rapids, but he knows this region far better than I do. Throughout high school, he regularly visited the Neck, and each December, he returns to take part in the Audubon Society's Christmas bird count.

On land still owned by the heirs of Henry K. Burgwyn —the boy colonel of the Confederacy who was killed at Gettysburg—we walk the ridges and swales formed by the meandering river. We shoot photographs of beaver ponds in the old oxbows and massive cotton fields on the higher ground. Some of the fields are so big and flat that they attract horned larks from the prairies and tundra. We stop at the abandoned store at Mud Castle and cross Occoneechee Creek, considered the true northern boundary of the Neck. On the fringes off US 158, we take pictures of the deteriorating home of Confederate general Matt Ransom. A few miles to the west, the lane into Longview Plantation was bordered, in my memory, by 200-year-old pines, but they have been recently cut.

As in William Faulkner's Mississippi, history and wildness lie close here. Yet it is clear that the Neck is not quite the foreboding place I'd imagined as a child. Except for the silver. Did it exist beyond the tattered pages of Mebane Burgwyn's *River Treasure,* the children's book I'd read and reread so many years earlier? Was it still deep in some oxbow flooded years ago by the Roanoke? Only she might know.

Her first reaction was to laugh gracefully when told her book was remembered fondly. Then she recounted this story: "My husband, John, and I first moved to the Neck about 1936. I was interested in writing at the time, and eventually wrote seven books. Three of those books, *River Treasure* (1947), *Lucky Mischief* (1949), and *Hunter's Hideout* (1959) were written about this area.

"Shortly after we arrived, John showed me a letter from an old man living in Maryland. It had been written to John's father, Henry Burgwyn. Among other things, the writer hinted that he knew the whereabouts of a chest of silver that had been buried by the Burgwyn family during the Civil War before Federal troops were turned back at a skirmish at Boone's Mill. We'd heard rumors of such a chest before, but no one had ever been able to confirm them.

"I showed the letter to some older folks living around Bull Hill on the western edge of the Neck where the Burgwyn homeplace had stood, and they told me that the old man in Maryland was in a mental institution—that I shouldn't pay any attention to him. In a second letter, the old man seemed more vague about locating the treasure, saying he'd need a 'divining rod' to find it. We didn't pursue it further, but I still have those letters somewhere."

"To this day, we don't know if the chest of silver ever existed, or if it did, whether it was found," she said. "But it was enough to give me an idea for a book, and that's how I came to write about a poor, young black boy who found buried silver here."

Surely, there will be times when I drive past Boone's Mill or down to Mud Castle again, most likely during holidays as before, and I'm sure I will still look off into those dense cypress and wonder. Could it be that Mebane's young hero may yet step through the top of a rotting chest?

TOUCH
AND GO
BOBWHITES

We separated to look for the dog, Mike Gaddis clambering through a cutover while I waded through a field of broom-straw that butted up against a dense wall of honeysuckle and greenbrier. It was not like Meg to be gone so long, unless she had found birds and was locked up somewhere ahead of us on point.

Finding a missing dog that's likely to be pointing birds is ticklish business. You don't want to leave a dog that's point-ing unfound too long, but you don't want to go rushing off dogless and blunder into other birds. It tends to work on the psyche—yours because what you've been hoping for might be just beyond the next tangle of briers; the dog's because it may have a snootful of the best smell in the world. Few bird dogs have a big enough tank to handle much of that volatile mixture without exploding.

I needn't have worried about Meg, however. Just about the time I heard Mike holler that she had checked in, I reached the edge of the field and walked into the biggest covey of bobwhites I'd seen on the farm in years. At least fif-teen blew out in a bunch and soared down the edge of the field, followed by three or four tail-end Charlies. I watched them go without shooting and saw them hook back into the woods, where they lit in dense ground cover just on the other side of a small creek.

"I'm sorry I got them up," I told Mike when he and Meg joined me, "but I saw right where they went." I should know better after all these years, but this time I was convinced that all Meg would have to do was hunt down the bottom, whereupon she would fetch up into a stylish point and Mike and I would walk in and flush the covey. Such delicious anticipation. Mike looked a bit skeptical. "Right there," I said, pointing, as Meg headed directly toward the spot, then ran past it without so much as a snuffle.

"Right back there," I said, dismayed, as Mike and I passed the spot and continued up the hill where Meg had gone. "Honest, I saw them sit down right there," I said. I kept looking at the ground as though I might see the covey still lounging there or detect signs of a hurried departure—a door left open, half-empty glasses, or an ashtray full of smoldering butts.

Welcome to the puzzling saga of quail hunting in the 1990s. It is a film noir, full of mysterious twists of plot and unexplained flashbacks. Nothing is as it seems, or ever was, least of all the quarry. All those lovely vintage calendar portraits of setters and pointers locked up in mid-field on bevies of tight-sitting quail are outright lies. If such a scene ever occurred, it happened only once and that was at least forty years ago. Mike knows this; Meg certainly does. I am the romantic who keeps hoping.

Biologists who specialize in small game say that the curious nontraditional habits of today's bobwhite quail are a function of changing or diminished habitat. There is also considerable evidence that loss of habitat has accelerated natural selection. Over the years, birds with the instincts to feed in the middle of a relatively open bean field were more likely to wind up in gravy over rice than their brethren who had a natural tendency to feed on wild seeds in thick bottomlands or cutovers. And those birds who haven't had their behavior adjusted by a load of number 8 shot have been educated or eliminated due to the relationship between lost habitat and a growing population of predators. At any rate, we're dealing with the Green Berets of bobwhites nowadays.

"If you were a quail, would you sit in the middle of a field under a dog's nose and wait for me to take a shot at you?" Mike asks. Point taken. A quail might, for laughs, wait for me to take a shot, figuring it would be low-risk entertainment, but only a daredevil would wait for Mike to do so.

"These birds wouldn't be here if they weren't adaptable, and a hunter who doesn't take that into account might as well sell his grandpa's old double and invest in antique calendars."

"So how come Meg didn't smell those birds?" I asked as Mike and I broke out of the thicket beyond the creek and began to work through a stand of young volunteer pines.

"I doubt if they ever lit, or if they did, they didn't stay long enough to leave much scent," he replied. "Probably they merely dipped low, then circled back somewhere and kept going. Or they ran, or lit in trees, or moved into condos and got jobs programming computers. Beats me; ask Meg."

We never found that covey, but we're still adapting. Meg's brother has recently become the proud father of a new litter of fresh troops, and we're counting on Sergeant Meg to tell her nieces and nephews what to expect. For sure, I can't.

COLLECTIONS
OUT OF
CONTROL

Have you priced any early handmade waterfowl decoys lately? How about older double-barrel shotguns or fishing lures, reels, or custom-built cane fly rods made before the 1950s? Sporting calendars, books, knives, license buttons? Unless you're already familiar with the values currently being assigned to these and countless other items of older hunting and fishing gear and associated memorabilia, you will be stunned at the prices being asked—and sometimes paid—for some of this stuff.

Not long ago, I was at a show where some high-priced duck decoys were being sold and was told by a collector that the best buy in the bunch was not one of the common Susquehanna Flats battery decoys at $500 or even one of the Outer Banks primitives at three times that price. It was a $20,000 decoy in original paint that had been carved by a well-known but underappreciated carver in the 1930s. It was, said my adviser, seriously underpriced.

"How seriously?" I asked.

"I'd say by at least half, possibly more," he replied. "That carver's skill is going to be even more fully recognized someday soon, and the price is going to skyrocket. Then the value will depend on the buyer."

I very carefully put it down since I did not want the value to depend on this particular buyer.

Over the past twenty years—and especially since the mid-1980s—well-heeled aficionados of sporting memorabilia have gone nuts collecting all the things that remind them of the golden age of hunting and fishing. Certainly much of it deserves to be collected and preserved because it was beau-

tifully made with careful handwork and a level of craftsman-
ship that approaches art. Even early commercially manufactured items often show remarkable design, skill, and high-
quality materials that give them great appeal.

Although all this interest has undoubtedly preserved
many of these items for future generations—items that
might otherwise have been tossed out in the trash—it is
cause for some sadness too. In the first place, when something generates interest and demand among collectors, it
is a pretty good indication that the activity associated with
it is in decline. We spend big bucks to set up museums full
of memorabilia to honor our waterfowl heritage along the
coast when we could be using that money to help preserve
the marshes and sounds that still support that resource.

Furthermore, the outlandish rise in values—much of it
purely for investment rather than for love of the sport—
dooms the casual collector who simply likes to have a few
of these things around to enjoy. How can you afford to go
bass fishing with a lure your grandfather left you after you
find out it's worth $50, or possibly a lot more? Those who
collect rare knives don't even sharpen them for fear of de-
stroying their value, and if you hunt with that old twenty-
gauge A-grade Parker double or fish with a Garrison cane
rod, you're risking the price of a college education at a private school.

Because investors have rapidly replaced true collectors,
they have driven values to outrageous levels. We're shocked
to discover that items someone may have given us ten years
ago now command such high prices that we are uncom-
fortable owning them. And since everyone seems to have
"heard" about these values, they put high prices on things
that are still virtually worthless. Just recently, I saw a pile
of beat-up plastic crankbaits at a flea market. Each lure was
tagged at $20, even though you could go next door to the
K-Mart and buy an identical new one for less than $5.

Those lures may never be worth more than retail, and
certainly not for many, many years. Indeed, despite the fact
that some sporting collectibles draw high prices, many old
sporting items still have little value. Bamboo rods are a good

example. There are millions of cheaply built cane casting and fly rods around that were mass-produced from about the 1920s until World War II, and most have very little value, even in mint condition. However, since the general public has read that a cane fly rod hand-built by one of a few notable craftsmen brought five figures at an auction, they assume that their rod is equally valuable. Try to convince them otherwise, and they think you're a common thief.

If you own sporting collectibles that you think may be valuable, my advice is to have them appraised and insure them. Then look for some other avenue to vent your collecting mania. Of course, I'm at a loss to suggest what you might substitute. At an antique tackle show, I recently saw a cased collection of tin split-shot boxes. You don't want to know how much the owner figured they were worth.

It all reminds me of the story of the fellow who told his friend that he owned a dog that was worth $10,000.

"How do you figure he's worth that much?" asked his friend.

"Well, that's easy," was the answer. "I traded two $5,000 cats for him."

MESSING AROUND IN SWAMPS

We didn't call them wetlands back when I was growing up in the 1940s and spending my summers at my grandparents' home in Northampton County. Grandmother, and everybody else, called such places bottoms or swamps, as in "Don't you mess around in that swamp, you hear me." I heard her all right, and most of the time I minded. Actually, it didn't take much to persuade me that the swamp might best be experienced from the outside — except for one time.

Grandmother's rambling frame house, with its embossed tin roof and wraparound porch, sat on low ground alongside US 258 just south of George, which is between Rich Square and Woodland. The huge front yard was so persistently wet that crayfish built mounds over much of it, but the real swamp was down behind the barn and half a mile through the woods to the back field, where the ground suddenly sloped off just beyond the soybeans into what was clearly a different kind of place. There were huge trees with swelled trunks and vines and roots and cypress knees to stumble over. At times, black water flooded it as far as I could see, and every time I stood in that field and looked deep into Urahaw Swamp, I felt an involuntary shiver. It was dark, impenetrable, infinite, and full of God knows what long before I was old enough to read or appreciate William Faulkner's descriptions of similar lowlands in Mississippi.

"You don't know what's in there," my grandmother told me. "People been in there and not come out. Some of Ed Lassiter's coon dogs never did. Something got 'em."

But I was curious. I had seen pterodactyls there, I was sure, and had heard their eerie cries. Sometimes when I was supposed to be playing in the barn loft, I would slip away to the back field and watch for flying dinosaurs. Even after I got a little older and realized that they were really only pileated woodpeckers, I was still fascinated by the swamp. Considering that some experts now think birds are descendants of dinosaurs, I might not have been totally off the mark.

Once, when I was about twelve, I was hunting squirrels with my uncle's single-shot .410 and decided to go into the swamp—just a little ways, of course. I wanted to hunt under those big trees full of squirrel nests that I could see maybe seventy-five yards away. The ground was fairly dry, and I wasn't afraid as long as I didn't think about it too much. I told myself I would walk straight to those trees, find a stump, and sit there until the squirrels forgot about me. But the nests turned out to be dense clumps of mistletoe, so I went a little farther before I found a good spot to wait.

I sat for a long time, and I remember having the exhilarating and uneasy feeling of being on the edge of something wild and unknowable. I could well believe that no one had ever perched on this particular stump—sawed it off, maybe, but not actually sat on it. Even so, that wonderful feeling of isolation was not misplaced because these large eastern swamps have seldom attracted many visitors except hunters, trappers, and loggers.

I had heard of the ghostly lady who was sometimes seen gliding across Lake Drummond in the Dismal Swamp, which wasn't too far away. Perhaps I would see a ghost. I might even see a bear, I thought happily. Then it occurred to me that a bear might also see me. Had that black stump over there really moved, or was it my imagination? Perhaps it was time to go. I hadn't seen any squirrels, and it was getting dark. I began to walk back in the direction of the field, pushing aside vines and trying to avoid the countless roots. After several minutes, I figured I should have come to the field. I stopped to look around a few yards from a pile of bare tree limbs. I didn't recall seeing them on the way in, but surely I would have noticed them. They were bleached so white that they looked like, like . . . bones . . . the bones of lost coon hounds! I didn't stop to see if they had treed a skeletal coon. Frantically, I stumbled forward, fighting my way through dense walls of greenbrier and switchcane. It was very nearly pitch dark now, and I was just about to decide that not even my bones would be found when I saw what appeared to be an opening ahead. I lunged through the last of the briers and stepped into a row of soybeans.

Ten minutes later, I was in my grandmother's warm kitchen, pinching pieces of crust off a platter of hot applejacks. Nobody asked where I'd been. I didn't tell.

In the years that followed, I spent a fair amount of time in lowlands and the edges of swamps in Halifax and Northampton Counties, mostly while hunting and fishing with my father and grandfather. Gum Swamp, Occoneechee Neck, and other wet bottomlands along the Roanoke, Cashie, and Chowan Rivers became less foreboding as they grew more familiar, but I could still sense their fertile mystery anytime I stared deep into the flooded cypress and tupelo.

It's doubtful that anyone would name a vast swamp "Dismal" these days because our attitudes toward such places have changed. For one thing, we no longer fear swamps as we once did and are less likely to think of them as havens of pestilence and unhealthy vapors. We know more about what lives there, and more important, we have learned that our various wetlands—large and small, wet and seemingly dry—hold the keys directly or indirectly to much of life on earth. Indeed, besides being nursery areas and homes for countless wildlife, our wetlands perform many invaluable services, ranging from providing flood control and filtering pollutants to replenishing water tables and favorably influencing our weather.

Even so, the outdated belief that wetlands are wastelands to be conquered still remains, and we continue to lose these valuable resources to drainage and conversion at an alarming rate. The issues are complex, particularly regarding private property rights, and even the very definition of a wetland is controversial. Indeed, it is possible that we will not all agree about the true value of wetlands until these resources are largely gone. If that happens, we will surely have lost priceless resources we now take for granted and perhaps we will even have threatened our very existence.

My grandmother told me not to mess around in the swamps nearly fifty years ago. "You don't know what's in there," she said. Her warning may be somewhat outdated for those who have learned to appreciate wetlands, but it's still good advice for those who might destroy them. After all, we know what's in there now.

THE
POINTER
OF NO
RETURN

Forget the traditional image of a brace of stylish English setters holding high, proud, and steady in an open field amid a blizzard of bobwhites. That's just another lovely lie. What I see instead is Buck, or rather Buck's rear end, disappearing rapidly as he races across a muddy field until he is a distant white dot.

There is also my increasingly agitated father, blowing his whistle and shouting, "Buck! Whoa Buck!" Repeated rapidly and punctuated with whistle blasts, it reminds me of some primal chant. When the white dot plunges into the worst thicket in both Carolinas, we stand quietly for a long time looking across the field. Finally, Dad turns to me and says, "I guess we better hunt in that direction."

Now, I probably ought to stop right here and explain that my purpose is not just to relate a series of tales about the most frustrating bird dog I've known in all my years of hunting. I could, to be sure, but I'm also interested in the covenant between bird dogs and their owners and the nature of an obsession that causes otherwise sane men and women to seek out and endure such an adversarial contract.

The glue that binds this unholy relationship is a complex substance, and I confess I know more about what it isn't than about what it is. Contrary to popular belief, it has nothing whatsoever to do with the bobwhite quail or any of its ilk. I have been on many hunts when bobwhites failed to participate, and in fact, I'm thrilled beyond all reason at a cameo appearance—a single bird flushing wild, for example. I take such happenings as evidence that quail are not, after all, extinct. But beyond that, quail are the least important part of this relationship.

Companionship in the field is one of the stock reasons hunters give for owning a bird dog, and I'll admit it's appealing to imagine the close teamwork of man and dog crossing fields and thick bottoms in relentless harmony. I have learned, however, that hunting with some dogs is about as companionable as playing chess by mail.

Buck entered the picture rather late since Dad and I had already spent years hunting with an assortment of bird dogs owned by my grandfather before he died in 1968. The doctor who sold him said Buck was about three years old and had a good nose. He also mentioned that Buck could cover a lot of ground quickly and never lost his intensity. Over the next dozen years, we found no reason to doubt that. To sweeten the deal, the doctor also threw in an unproven setter named Sam.

Together, Buck and Sam perfected the "flying point." Sam was always jealous of every covey Buck pointed, so he simply refused to honor Buck's point. Sam would creep forward and Buck would roll his eyes sideways, appalled at this blatant attempt to steal his covey. Then he, too, would begin to creep. The creep would become a trot, the trot a canter, and within moments, both dogs would be side by side at full gallop, tails held high as though they believed the birds would stick tight as long as style was not abandoned. We saw lots of birds that year, but we seldom had a target unless you count the times when Sam proved almost too tempting to pass up.

After Sam was placed on waivers the following spring, Dad set about trying to find a way to encourage Buck to hunt a little closer. We knew that he could find birds; we just wanted him to find some in the same county we planned to hunt. A twenty-foot cord proved ineffective. Hooking one of Buck's forelegs under his collar sounded like a good idea when someone first suggested it, but we quickly learned that Buck still had a leg up on us. Dangling a heavy chain from his collar to break his stride showed some early promise until Buck learned to adjust his gait to something that resembled a breaststroke and "swam" out of sight as usual.

Over the course of one season, Buck's collar sported a sequence of increasingly larger bells until he looked like a small Guernsey. Dad finally concluded that the only bell that might work would have to come out of Notre Dame Cathedral. Despite all these efforts, at times we saw Buck only twice during the day—when we turned him loose and again after dark when the lone ranger would reappear at the car with a wagging tail and a look that plainly said, "Gee, I had a great time and found lots of birds. Hope you guys found some too." Then he'd roll in a cow pie to freshen up and hop into the backseat to enjoy the ride home.

Late one afternoon while we were waiting at the car for Buck to show up, Dad told me of a dream he'd had the night before. "You know, I've been yelling at Buck for six years now, and once he's in the field he doesn't pay any more attention to me than if I were the man in the moon. Last night, I dreamed I was feeding him and he was jumping up and down like he always does, and his head hit me in the chin. I bit off my tongue, and when it fell out on the ground, Buck ate it."

"I think," I said, "it may be time for you to try one of those training shock collars before this dog puts you in the loony bin."

It never occurred to me that Dad, being a gentle soul, would first try it on himself. An unimpeachable source—Mom—reported to me a week or so later that Dad had been wandering around in the yard wearing the new collar.

"Well, he wanted to make sure it wasn't actually going to hurt Buck, you know, so he gave me the controls and told me to zap him at various distances," she said. "I've got him coming around pretty well now, but I don't think it's helped his nose a bit."

It would be refreshing to be able to report that the shock collar convinced Buck to become the close-hunting companion we'd always envisioned, but that was not to be. Buck quickly learned, as we had hoped, that he could avoid being zapped as long as he stayed within a certain distance. But he also figured out by trial and error that the range of that collar was limited. From the moment Buck learned this, he automatically adjusted his field work into three zones— watch your step, the border, and free at last. No national champion ever hunted better inside of a hundred yards, cutting and circling and putting on a show, but after about twenty minutes, when Buck figured you were relaxing your vigil, his circles would gradually get wider and wider until he was cruising at the edge of the collar's range. He knew he was only yards away from pay dirt, and once he'd gotten that far, you couldn't have forestalled the inevitable if you'd plugged his tail directly into a socket.

Suddenly, Buck would bolt for the border in a cloud of dust. Driven by a fading current of electricity and accompanied by a chorus of "whoas," he'd soon be out of sight.

"Have you considered carrying a backpack generator to power that thing?" I recall asking Dad once after we'd witnessed one of Buck's escapes with a mixture of frustration and admiration. The truth is that Dad never took any of this personally. He never hit Buck or even scolded him very sharply, and as the years passed, it was clear that they had reached an understanding. Buck would hunt the way he wanted to hunt, and Dad would let him. Even in my youthful impatience, I could see the wisdom of such an arrangement. I've never seen a closer bond develop between man and dog, and on the happy and rare occasions when a bird intruded, the rewards were unparalleled.

I recall one brisk November day when Dad happened to knock down a bobwhite in a thicket on the backside of the Granville County farm. At the shot, Buck characteristically evaporated to look for singles. (In all fairness, we had rarely given him any reason to expect something so miraculous as a downed bird.) Dad called again and again, but it was apparent that if the bird was to be—as the game wardens say— reduced to possession, we would have to do the reducing.

I buttoned up my jacket, jammed on my cap, and crawled into the thickest infestation of catbrier, honeysuckle, and grape vines between Hudson Bay and Cape Horn. Ten minutes later, I had pretty well searched an area the size of a phone booth. It was evident that without the aid of tin snips, it would take another ten minutes just to turn around.

Then I heard something plowing through the brush and Buck came breaststroking past me trailing his chain. He was panting like a steam engine, and his cowbell clanged with every lunge.

"Thatta boy, Buck, go get 'em boy," cried Dad, his voice nearly delirious with unexpected delight. "Dead bird, Bucky. Dead bird, Bucky puppy. Look at that. Would ya look at that sweet ol' puppy dog."

After I managed to extract myself from the edge of the thicket, Dad and I stood in awe for ten minutes listening to brush crunching, limbs cracking, and an assortment of snuffles, clangs, grunts, and yelps. We couldn't have been more surprised when Buck finally staggered free of the thicket, his tail and flanks raked by briers, his belly and legs black with mud, and his mouth full of bobwhite.

Dad said, and I believed him, that he wouldn't take $1,000 for that moment.

As Buck grew old and increasingly feeble, Dad kept a diary, entering each hunt and compiling them into an annual chapter that he mailed to me and my brothers at the end of each season. It reads more like the adventures of two close old friends than a mere log of hunting dates, coveys pointed, and birds shot at. I found the following entry in the 1983 edition, written when Buck was sixteen and Dad was sixty-seven: "I'm afraid this might have been Buck's last hunt. He knows every inch of this farm, every place he's ever found birds, but he didn't run at all this trip. He just walked along, sometimes to one side and sometimes a little in front. He doesn't see too well, and he hears more poorly than ever. I used to wonder if his lack of attention was because of poor hearing or his great power of concentration or whether it was just plain stubbornness. Whatever it was when he was younger, I know it's hearing now. I'm afraid to remove the bell for if he should get out of sight, I might never find him. He moves so slowly that the bell barely tinkles, but he still loves to hunt. I keep thinking of all the past hunts, and I'll bet Buck does too. Somehow, I feel we both think alike. I know we both like the same things."

Buck is gone now, and in all honesty, for a while I sort of figured that Dad's enthusiasm might have followed. But I was wrong. Jake is coming along nicely, and though he hunts much more closely than Buck ever did, he's developing his own sense of style. Last year, he came prancing through the woods with his first bird and deposited it proudly at Dad's feet. It was a slightly gummed, but otherwise unharmed, chicken.

STILL
WORTH
THE
TROUBLE

The hardwoods along the rural Granville County blacktops were nearing peak color one day this past fall when Dad and I stopped to see Mike Gaddis. Ladybugs were everywhere, dust motes drifted in the bright sun, and the woods had a hot, dry smell. We walked down the path to Mike's kennels, where he proudly showed off his latest year-old litter of English setters, all licks, leaps, and love. Meg and Sir came out of their barrels to greet us but stood quietly with the dignity befitting their thirteen years.

Was it just last January or the one before that Meg had found that covey behind the cabin in the low cover between the thick hedgerow of shrub lespedeza and the woods? Her staunch point in the first vaporous swirls of light snow had been steady even amid the thundering rush of a dozen bobwhites.

As Dad and I followed Mike back to the car, we passed the graveyard where a dozen or more stones are carefully arranged in the woods, each bearing the name of a dog. I know them: Squaw, Mutt, Pat, Cindy, and the others.

Mike, at one point, was not certain that he and Loretta would raise and train another litter, even at the risk of losing the line of breeding that had served them so many years and so well. It was not just the inevitable sadness of losing such close companions every ten to fifteen years; it was the realization that any new setter or pointer, regardless of its innate and learned skills, has far fewer opportunities to prove itself on wild birds these days.

But when Mike speaks of dogs, past and present, it is clear

that there's far more involved than hunting. He loves the sweet smell of puppy breath, the sharp teeth on bare ankles, the bold and awkward inquisitiveness, and that first tentative point when a young dog is introduced to a quail wing tethered to a bamboo pole. Again and again, Mike has seen intelligence, trust, and loyalty grow into an unmeasurable desire to please. But more than any of this, he is forever astonished by the near-human—and sometimes hilarious— ways dogs relate to their two-legged companions.

"I had a dog—Beda was her name—that had wonderful qualities, but she had one flaw as a young dog," Mike recalls. "She quickly learned my limitations, and if she observed that I had momentarily lost sight of her, she would take off to hunt alone. She found plenty of birds and undoubtedly had a great time, but she preferred that I not get in the way."

"It was a trait that needed a quick remedy before it became a ruinous habit. Fortunately, I had just begun to experiment with dog training using telemetry," he said. "With a hand-carried radio and a small transmitter on the collar, you can track the exact location of the dog. The first time I used that system, Beda had run off as usual and I suspected she was pointing a distant covey. When I showed up a few minutes later, the shocked look on her face was priceless. I know she was thinking, 'How did he do that?'

"After I quickly tracked her down several times, you could see her figuratively throw her paws up in the air as if to say, 'Well, dang, here he is again. I guess I'm gonna have to hunt with the so-and-so.'"

Mike's story reminds me of a pointer named Frank that belonged to my grandfather's brother. The brother seldom missed a bird, whereas my grandfather seldom hit one—a singular lack of skill that he has passed on to his son, and his son, and mine (there's no escape, alas, from the destiny of linebreeding). One day, Granddad borrowed Frank for a hunt, but every time Frank pointed and the birds got up, my grandfather missed with both barrels.

Finally, after Granddad missed an easy, near-gliding, straightaway shot across an open field on the fourth covey,

Frank turned and looked at him. Then he headed straight for the house, ignoring every call and whistle. When my grandfather got there, Frank was hiding under the porch and wouldn't come out.

As for Dad, his beloved Buck died years ago. He was followed a dozen years later by Jake, a puppy from one of Mike's earlier litters. It was like losing members of the family. Dad said he simply couldn't endure that again, so he's been without a dog for years.

Now he says he's too old for another dog, but I'm not quite sure of that. I saw the way he looked at those puppies.

BREAKFAST
FOR
SUPPER

It was well below freezing and still dark when my grand-father and I pulled up to the Kings' house at the Granville County farm, but I was not surprised to see a light on in the kitchen. When we stepped inside, a blast of heat greeted us. Everyone was up and dressed—had already been to the barn, in fact—and Mr. King was sitting at the head of the table eating a breakfast of navy beans, homemade barbe-cue, and scratch biscuits made with lard. Some biscuits were dripping with molasses, and some were clamped around thick chunks of fried fatback. I noted that Mr. King was also crumbling biscuits in black coffee and drinking it thick. It looked and smelled powerful good to a thirteen-year-old boy with two hollow legs who hadn't had anything to eat in at least an hour, and it didn't take much prodding for me to pull up a chair.

I have long forgotten anything about the quail hunting that day. I can't even recall whether anyone went with us or which dogs did what. But I haven't forgotten Mr. King's breakfast. Odd as it may sound, it was not a particularly un-usual country breakfast back then—not substantially differ-ent from countless others I have eaten in the homes of rela-tives across a rural swath of eastern North Carolina from Granville to Halifax to Northampton County. And you can throw in similar predawn, jump-start engorgements with hunting and fishing companions all over the state.

Pardon me if I'm wrong, but it seems we are in danger of misplacing breakfast—at least the kind that features animal fat, cholesterol, calories, and caffeine. Some of us don't par-take of breakfast at all, and the rest are nowadays more likely to nibble a bit of fruit and toast a bagel or slop a half cup of skim milk over some dried twigs and wheat chaff. That might be good for the heart, but it doesn't speak to the soul.

It wasn't always this way. Not so many years ago, the kitchen was the heart of any house—especially any farmhouse. For one thing, at four o'clock in the morning in winter, it was likely to be the only room in the house with any heat in it. Indeed, the front rooms in most farmhouses, with their black horsehair sofas, were open only for weddings and funerals (old farmers never die, they just close up the rest of the house and live beside the cookstove). And when you live in a kitchen and rise before daylight, breakfast probably isn't a Pop Tart.

It may be premature to mourn the passing of the country breakfast, but just in case, let's light a candle and hold a brief service. And, yes, I'll wait while you get your bib.

The first item likely to be on any plate is a scratch biscuit made of flour, lard, and sweet milk or buttermilk. I suppose this has always been the essential centerpiece, but let me recommend a variation. It has been many years since I had one of my grandmother's clabber biscuits. She milked the cow and kept the unhomogenized milk in the refrigerator until it soured, then used this clabber to make sourdough. The biscuits were big and fluffy, just the thing to spread with molasses, homemade jelly, jam, preserves, or butter (never margarine). If it was girth you were after, you'd stuff a clabber biscuit with a slab of country ham, fried fatback, sausage, scrapple, bacon, or country-fried steak. And if you really wanted to test your galluses, you'd split a pile of biscuits on a large platter and smother them in redeye or sausage gravy.

Another bit of breakfast magic rarely encountered today is the crackling biscuit (small bits of fried pork fat are added to the dough). I would not say that I would kill for a crackling biscuit, but I might maim.

Of course, there were fresh eggs when the hens were laying, but eggs were fried hard or sunny-side up—seldom scrambled and almost never poached. I remember that my Northampton County grandmother would discard the whites from soft-fried eggs until she had a pile of yolks. Then she'd crumble bacon and toast crumbs over them, mash everything into a paste, and eat it with a fork. She was, understandably, just about as wide as she was tall, but she was happy in her work and her soul was well fed.

Another breakfast item that seems to have fallen out of favor is the sweet potato—baked, split while hot, then slathered in butter and mashed with a fork. Rare was the wood cookstove that didn't have leftover sweet potatoes, biscuits, and corn bread lined up behind the ever-present pot of coffee, and rarer still was the person headed for the field who didn't stick a sampling in his overalls.

Sometimes breakfast would also include a special treat like flapjacks (invariably soaked in Karo syrup), toasted pound cake, or salt-rising bread. But muffins and waffles were fairly rare. Like French toast, they seemed to belong to another social strata.

Nutritionists have always told us that breakfast is the most important meal of the day, but they now say we shouldn't eat this stuff. So where does that leave us?

I don't know about you, but I'm going to resurrect a tradition from my childhood. I'm gonna start eating breakfast for supper.

THE
GHOSTS
OF
CHRISTMAS

Christmas almost got past me again last year. It has been that way for some time. Nowadays, the holiday more often arrives in bits and pieces, catching me off guard in unlikely places. Some years, it hasn't appeared until after the twenty-fifth. This is disconcerting to someone who, as a child, used to cultivate a rampant tingle of seasonal goodwill and anticipation long before the jack-o'-lantern had rotted into a blackened lump on the porch.

Reason suggests that this is nothing more than a natural by-product of growing older. At a certain age, children can hardly expect to go back to the house they grew up in and find it filled with family and colored lights overlaid with the mingled scents of evergreen, fragrant candles, hot turkey, roasted pecans, sweet ambrosia, and dark fruitcake. Even if we're fortunate to still spend holidays with loved ones, it is often in places that have no intimate past for us, and we go and return along unfamiliar routes. This doesn't mean that Christmas has been lost, only that it no longer has such a palpable presence.

Two years ago, my Christmas showed up on the afternoon of the twenty-third in a rural farm supply store. I was on the way to the farm and in a hurry, and I had stopped to look for colored outdoor bulbs. It's an old place filled with hardware, farm gear, tools, gardening supplies, seed, and fertilizer. You pay for things inside a smaller, much warmer, partitioned area in the back, where shelves and walls are stacked and hung with boots, clothing, and general merchandise. Since the holiday was imminent, there were also a few toys, jars of preserves, and candy.

The person ahead of me, a burly man in overalls and a grimy cap, had assembled a small pile on the counter. He looked a bit desperate, and twice he apologized to those of us behind him.

"It's not enough," I heard him mumble to himself. I glanced over his shoulder and saw a box of coconut flag candy, a bag of malted milk balls, some English walnuts, a small pair of red cowboy boots, a cap pistol in a silver-studded white leather holster, and a doll in a box that made it appear as though she were looking through the curtains at a window.

"I got 'em all covered but one, I think," he said to the clerk. "I still need a big item for the littlest boy."

I suddenly had the strange sensation that it was Christmas in 1950. The setting fit, and all the characters were straight out of a Norman Rockwell painting. We were a cliché, watching this one-stop, last-minute shopper buying Santa Claus in a country store, no doubt with the last of the egg money. I began to look around. We all did, hopeful that we might be able to help him fill out his list. People scattered to inspect the shelves and offer suggestions. It didn't occur to me that some might have been motivated simply by the desire to get him out of the way. Blue jeans were rejected (too everyday), an air rifle was waved off (kid's too young), a red bandanna was put back (too cheap), and a straw cowboy hat was declined (too big for his head).

"Here you go," someone said, handing the man a box containing a small cast-iron replica of a Farmall tractor, complete with plow, spreader, and disc.

"Ring it up," said the father with relief as everyone cheered. "It's perfect."

It was perfect, so perfect that I was stunned. Was this déjà vu or a full-length movie? You see, I had once received an identical tractor, and that Christmas I had plowed the frozen hardpan in the backyard and disced the entire sand-box with it. The following spring, I used it to plow a two-foot-square garden where I planted radishes, one of which actually came up. When I left the store, I half expected to see the streets white with snow and filled with mule-drawn wagons and 1940s vintage Fords and Chevys.

Christmas has caught me off guard in other recent years. In 1993, it appeared in a wistful moment as my son Scott and I stopped along the roadside at dusk to watch a "V" of Canada geese that flew high over the flat winter fields near Lake Mattamuskeet. On the curve of the horizon, a smear of colored lights shone in the window of a dark farmhouse, calling up visions of forty years of preholiday hunts, a peanut-eating black Lab, icy dawns, and a father and grandfather teasing a half-frozen youngster who had just shot his first goose.

On the heel of this past December, the holiday came on a raw wind in late afternoon as three hunters walked a row of rattling soybeans. The setter ranged ahead, clearly tiring but still looking for the sundown covey. "Do you smell ham cooking?" I asked. "No? I could have sworn I smelled country ham just now. And cedar. Don't you smell the cedar?"

Yes, they smelled the cedar. We stopped and stood together, savoring this season and the many before it.

A RECIPE FOR CHRISTMAS

We drove down to Mattamuskeet four days before Christmas. It was not going to be the same—I knew that—but I was hoping I would be the only one to notice. Beginning with my late grandfather and father in the 1950s, a preholiday trip to this fabled waterfowl hunting spot has been part of family tradition. Some years, we have only looked at the Canadas and ducks or resorted to secondary plans to hunt off the lake somewhere, but it has always turned out to be special in some indefinable way. This year, at least, we had drawn a blind.

Dad had decided to forego the trip because he felt he would not be able to get to and from the blinds as he once had, and my brother Graham ran into a last-minute conflict. So for the first time, there were only three of us—my brother John, my son Scott, and myself. Mom, though she never hunted, had always cooked our ducks or geese for a festive holiday feast, but she had died in 1992. And John's wonderful old Lab Sanford was no longer with us either.

Yet we were off to a promising start. Ella Fitzgerald and Louis Armstrong were singing "Have Yourself a Merry Little Christmas" when we pulled in near Rose Bay to buy a bushel of oysters. When we crossed the causeway, flocks of geese and ducks were flying against the red sunset. Small groups bobbed along the bulrushes, and we could see large rafts of resting waterfowl farther out, mere dark patches against the reflected light. Our room was waiting at Mrs. Sadler's in Fairfield, and the big cedar on the corner in front of the store sparkled with big colored lights.

We hunted the following morning in a dense fog with the lake as calm as oilcloth on a kitchen table. No ducks flew early, and after a warm sun burned off the mist, we stood in the blind and listened to the distant flutelike calls of resting swans. But there was always tomorrow. And besides, it had been years since we had hunted more than memories anyway. Just being in duck country was enough to bring high spirits.

The afternoon was so unseasonably warm—in the mid-70s—that we pulled up lawn chairs beside the motel, retrieved the bushel of oysters from the shade, and set to work with oyster knives, slurping the cool, salty oysters with a dab of Tabasco, then cleansing our pallets with nips of sixteen-year-old single malt. 'Twas fine, indeed, but the bright orange tabby that joined us spurned all our efforts to get him to eat an oyster. How odd, we thought. John's Lab had loved raw oysters, even with hot sauce and horseradish.

Then Scott disappeared for a few moments, returning with two pie pans.

"I thought these might be appreciated," he said as he peeled back the tinfoil on a pair of chess pies. "I made them using that old recipe that was always our favorite when we were growing up. You know the one, don't you?"

Indeed, we did. That chess pie recipe had come from my great-grandmother. Two years before my mother died, she had asked me what I wanted for Christmas that year. "All I want is for you to write down the old family recipes," I said. She had had a time converting smidgens and pinches of lard, flour, and other ingredients into standard measurements for all those old recipes, but the result has proven to be one of the best legacies she left us.

That evening, contentedly full of oysters and pie, we walked into the banding site on the southeast corner of the huge lake just to look. In that vast amphitheater, we could barely hear each other speak amid the cacophony of quacks and honks as vast flocks of snow geese and tight, fast bunches of ducks passed overhead.

Late that night, the wind came up, swinging out of the southwest. By the time we got settled in the blind the next morning, a pretty good chop had our decoys dancing. Scott fell in—upholding another family tradition—but the water was shallow and he said it wasn't cold. We knew better, but ducks were flying. We missed them (tradition dies hard). More flew; we missed them too. Then Scott made a fine passing shot on a drake pintail.

"That's enough," we agreed, and we retrieved our decoys. It was more than enough. Another holiday was upon us, rich as always, even richer because there were still three pieces of pie left for the trip home.

This Christmas, if you are fortunate enough to have the opportunity, ask for those recipes in the handwriting you will always remember.

MERCURY
BIRDS

The weeks had been flying by, and it was already past Christmas—two days past New Year's even—and we had not yet had a real bird hunt. It was the same old story: obligations, holiday schedules, missed opportunities, uninviting weather. Mike Gaddis and I had tried it a couple of times, but it had been unseasonably warm, and Mike's dog, Meg, had informed us that she didn't keep company with sweaty quail. At any rate, she declined to introduce us to any.

But now the weather was perfect—cold, gray, still, solemn. By the time Mike and Meg joined my son Scott and me at my cabin at the farm, I had already built a good oak fire in the woodstove, then choked it down with the damper so it would slowly warm the cabin while we hunted. The NuGrape soda sign thermometer in the kitchen read 30 degrees. A bobwhite would surely smell sweet today.

Bear in mind that our expectations were limited. Mike and I are at an age—both in years and in our realization of changing times—at which hunting is broadly defined and sometimes doesn't even involve game. Though much younger, Scott has been linebred to that same point of view. Grandfathers may no longer join us, but we are wearing their clothes, carrying their shotguns, and following the off-spring of their dogs. On those rare occasions when the birds know what is expected of them, we hang up the memory like an old sporting calendar and look at it for years.

The first covey got up wild in the thick pines behind Estore's long-abandoned house and flew toward the distant bottom. We had not expected to find birds there, and Meg had never even gotten close enough to pick up a scent. But we decided to look for the singles and followed Meg through the woods past the rusty hulk of a 1949 Mercury. I stopped a moment to look at the car. I had shot my first bobwhite over that abandoned car so many years ago that the tall pines I was standing under had been a field. I was about to point it out to Scott and Mike.

"You're going to tell us about that bird again, aren't you?" Scott teased gently. "It's on the tip of your tongue. I can see the little wheels turning. What would it take for you to pass this pile of junk once without mentioning that poor bob-white? We'll pay."

"Handsomely," Mike added, laughing. I grumbled some-thing about the general lack of respect among younger gen-erations, but to no avail. They know me too well. Besides, with the real thing at hand, Meg wasn't waiting to hear about any forty-year-old ghosts. Already, she was a white blur bouncing through the distant switchcane at the edge of the bottom. Meg looked long and hard, but like so many woods coveys, our birds had executed some fancy wingwork and disappeared.

We hunted across several dense bottoms and skirted some likely field edges without success, then in late after-noon under an increasingly sullen sky, we began to work our way back toward the cabin. Ahead of us lay a sloping field that had been converted from cropland to wildlife food and cover under the federal Conservation Reserve Program. Hedgerows of shrub lespedeza crisscrossed the hip-deep grass and broomstraw, and on the side of the hill, Meg stood in a classic open-field point. We stopped in stunned admiration.

"Hold back until I get on the upper side, then we'll go in together," whispered Mike. "Move quickly, but deliberately, and no talking. Let's go."

This time, the covey sat tightly under Meg's proud nose, then flushed tightly packed in a thunder of wings.

"I got one," shouted Scott. "Me too," Mike and I both echoed. When Meg, unaccountably, could find only one bird, we began to reconstruct our shots and the plot thinned. Out of some dozen quail, we had all shot the same bird. "I think that's called conservation," Mike observed.

"Well, I believe I hit another one on my second shot," said Scott. We followed Meg nearly fifty yards into the woods before she pointed again and Scott collected his bird. It was his first double—despite shared honors—and he marked the spot by placing the empty shellcase over the stub of a limb.

"This is one day you'll always remember," I told him. "Like me and my Mercury bird, you may have the pleasure of telling your children and grandchildren how it happened, and where, until they're all sick of hearing about it."

"And you can tell them it began to snow too," Mike added, pointing out the first falling flakes. We left the woods and walked through the swirling snow thinking, what could be more perfect?

Only this. That eight wood ducks flew overhead just as we reached the cabin. That Mike was so deliriously happy that he said he could wallow on the ground (and did so while we held his gun). That we ate dried raisins—the old-fashioned kind still on the stem—as I lit the oil lamps in the cabin. That as we were unloading our gear, the setting sun appeared suddenly under a ragged bank of dark snow clouds and lit the fields and falling snow in soft, warm light. Or that, incredibly, a rainbow (snowbow?) appeared overhead.

We stood speechless before the amazing spectacle, afraid even to blink, as—unwrapped, unexpected, and undeserved—the best gift of the holiday season was delivered.

JOE'S
FRIENDS

Back in the late 1970s, I was fishing a trout stream that wound through a small community tucked into a deep fold between heavily forested mountains. It was a dozen miles of single-lane gravel from any pavement. There was an old store, a church, a handful of small houses and cabins, a converted rusty bus or two, and the stream. I had discovered that this stretch held a few wild browns that had learned to dodge the summer swimmers and the hotdogs and corn tossed their way by hopeful kids, and when time was short or I was too lazy to walk to a remote stream, it posed an interesting challenge.

That day, I came around a bend near the church and saw that a baptism was taking place several pools above me. I considered that it would be improper to fish through the middle of the ceremony, and the trout—freshly washed in blessings of renewal—would probably not be taking communion again anyway. I had no wish to intrude, so I left quietly.

This past New Year's Day, I stood shivering with the others on top of the hill behind the church. We had followed the hearse up the icy road, and now we were gathered in a semicircle while a young woman sang "Amazing Grace" for Joe McDade. How strange it felt to be there—no doubt, strange for all of us. It seemed that Joe and Elaine and I had just cooked supper on the Coleman stove in my cabin, though it had been two months ago. He and I were going to fish the Watauga and South Holston in Tennessee in the spring and have hamburgers and shakes for lunch at the Classic Malt Shop in Elizabethton. We were considering a pilgrimage to Pennsylvania's limestone streams. He would surely be climbing my steps that evening to fetch me over to Ben Hartley's to watch Ben feed his deer. Or we'd be out keeping the "big eye" peeled for who knows what—it's a blood sport in a place with a handful of permanent residents and longtime interlopers like me. Or maybe we'd just sit on the porch and talk. But Joe suddenly dead at fifty-eight?

Many of us on that windy hill behind the church had fished and hunted with Joe through the years, had learned from him, had come to appreciate his wry humor, had trusted his friendship and kindness. We had also found a depth that went far beyond the shared interest of angling. I knew he'd had some rough years earlier, but he had found his home here. He had met Elaine Gentry, and they had joined a church and were making plans. Some of the best fruit ripens late, and this seemed to be true of them.

I was pleased to see that Joe would be buried next to Archie and Buena Coffey. He would have liked that because Archie, who had owned the store, had befriended Joe when he was a kid just learning to fish. I turned and looked across the creek toward Yellowbuck Mountain, then upstream to a rocky cliff high above the store on Yancy Ridge. Joe would surely have appreciated this eternal view overlooking a creek still pure enough to hold wild trout.

I could see the pool where I had witnessed the baptism all those years ago, and I remembered how Joe had laughed when I told him that I had caught and released a small brown trout later that very afternoon near where the preacher had stood.

"Saved by grace, man and fish," we had agreed. It had seemed to us so perfectly in tune with nature, this notion that we are all caught and released many times until we are finally kept.

I thought of the many friends who had been connected to that creek and community since that opening day in 1967 when my dear old buddy A. J. Johnson had first invited me to his cabin. Johnson, who taught me so much about trout fishing, had died at the age of eighty-eight in 1993. Gone, too, was Ben, our tough-gentle, humorous companion, dead these two years. And of course it was not lost on me that I, too, was fifty-eight. The valley seemed filled with the mingled presence of the living and the dead, with no clear distinction between us anymore.

I didn't know whether I could fish those waters again so soon, but when A. J.'s son Alvin called to say that opening day would be observed at the cabin as usual this past April, I went anyway. In that familiar place, I discovered that whereas once I had been the youngest, I was now the oldest. But I felt spirits moving among us—"once lost, now found"—and they were clearly passing their infectious love of those mountains, streams, and trout to a new generation.

We fished, and our luck was very, very good.